Six Axes Astrology

Six Axes Astrology
The zodiac in 6 axes instead of 12 signs or how your opposite sign completes you
Author: © Benjamin Adamah
2023

Lay-out: www.burokd.nl
ISBN 978-94-92355-60-7

Published by:

VAMzzz Publishing
P.O. Box 3340
1001 AC Amsterdam
The Netherlands
www.vamzzz.com
vamzzz@protonmail.com

SIX AXES
ASTROLOGY

THE ZODIAC IN 6 AXES INSTEAD OF 12 SIGNS
OR HOW YOUR OPPOSITE SIGN COMPLETES YOU

BENJAMIN ADAMAH

Contents

Introduction

Many people have read about their zodiac sign, but few realize the importance of understanding the sign that is opposite to their Sun. By gaining insight into this opposite sign, you can avoid many problems, delays, opposition, and blockages that may arise in your life. For instance, Aries individuals can improve their chances of success and happiness by integrating the qualities of Libra, and vice versa. Similarly, the combination of Taurus-Scorpio, Gemini-Sagittarius, Cancer-Capricorn, Leo-Aquarius, and Virgo-Pisces can benefit from a deeper understanding of their opposite sign. By embracing the lessons and traits of these opposite signs, one can attain greater harmony and balance in their life. While most people know their zodiac sign, many still view astrology as a nonsensical superstition. However, there are two reasons for this misconception that I'd like to point out.

Firstly, the horoscopes found in magazines, newspapers, and on astro-tv are not representative of true astrology. As an example, during a period when I was dedicating 18 hours per week to bodybuilding, I once came across a horoscope in magazine that read: "You really need to get into sports a little more, lazy Taurus!" Such nonsense is never written by serious astrologers. Additionally, the terms "weekly" or "monthly horoscope" are misnomers as they offer only generalized "forecasts" or phantasies of the person who writes them. In order to take astrology seriously, a proper analysis must be conducted based on an individual's birth chart, progressions, solar returns, and current planetary aspects, including asteroids and sensitive points like the Black Moon, Lunar Nodes, etc.

The second cause is far more insidious. When you ask people about their "star sign" (which is also a misnomer as it refers to a sign and not a constellation), they typically respond with statements like "I am a Gemini," "I am a Virgo," "I am a Sagittarius," or "I am a Leo", etc. What makes this response so problematic? Well, the position of the Sun (your "I") at the time of your birth indicates which zodiac sign it was in, but this is just one of many factors that determine your character, being, and individuation process. Your Sun sign is always opposed by the sign that *complements* its qualities and wants to integrate into your personality. Unfortunately, most people initially perceive this opposing sign as a counter-force. For example, Libras may view Aries as egoists who always get in their way, Taurians may see Scorpions as only interested in power and manipulation, and Capricorns may find Cancers to be hypersensitive emotional complainers, etc. This type of thinking stems from a deeply flawed view of reality, the concept of duality. However, duality is a human invention. In astrology and nature, there is no such thing as duality.

Just as an artist knows that yellow enhances shades of purple (which opposes yellow on the color-wheel), we must learn to bring together seemingly opposite elements of our birth chart. Rather than working with only 12 signs, we can focus on the 6 axes of 2 signs each, which complement and reinforce one another. By studying the sign that is opposite to our own, we can gain valuable insights into our character, life, and destiny. It's important to note that this approach is often ignored by many astrologers, but it can provide much more workable knowledge than a classic horoscope interpretation. Ultimately, learning to bring these complementary elements into synergy is the key to unlocking the full potential of our birth chart.

THE SIX ZODIACAL AXES ARE:

1. **Aries – Libra axis**: Aries represents the self and Libra represents the other. By balancing the needs of the self and the needs of others, individuals can create harmonious relationships and avoid conflicts.
2. **Taurus – Scorpio axis**: Taurus represents stability and Scorpio represents transformation. By embracing change and adapting to new situations, individuals can achieve greater stability and security.
3. **Gemini – Sagittarius axis**: Gemini represents communication and Sagittarius represents exploration. By communicating effectively and seeking new experiences, individuals can expand their knowledge and understanding of the world.
4. **Cancer – Capricorn axis**: Cancer represents emotions and Capricorn represents practicality. By balancing emotions with practicality, individuals can achieve their goals while maintaining a healthy emotional state.
5. **Leo – Aquarius axis**: Leo represents individuality and Aquarius represents community. By expressing their individuality while also contributing to their community, individuals can achieve personal fulfillment while making a positive impact on the world.
6. **Virgo - Pisces axis**: Virgo represents analysis and Pisces represents intuition. By combining analytical thinking with intuition, individuals can make better decisions and achieve greater understanding of themselves and the world around them.

Overall, the complementary nature of these zodiacal axes allows you to integrate your unconscious self and achieve greater balance and productivity in your live.

We were discussing the significance of the Sun's position in the horoscope. However, it's important to approach the Moon, ascendant, and ruling planet with the same level of importance, along with the other ingredients in your natal chart. The Sun, Moon, and ascendant are considered the three most significant components of a birth chart in astrology. The Sun represents one's *core identity*, *life purpose*, and *ego*, while the Moon symbolizes *emotions*, *feelings*, and *instincts*. The ascendant, also known as the rising sign, reflects our *outer personality*, *first impression*, and *how we appear to others*. These three elements are interconnected in a birth chart, and their placement in the chart can provide insight into one's personality traits, strengths, weaknesses, and potential challenges in life. The combination of the Sun, Moon, and ascendant can also reveal a person's overall temperament, inner motivations, and life goals.

While you can typically determine your Sun, Moon, and ascendant on your own, the remaining data processing is best left to a professional. Our journey towards self-awareness, from birth to death, involves a process of defragmentating our minds and becoming complete. This entails reintegrating the things that were excluded, or in a sense, put on hold at the time of our birth, so that we can exist as a whole new individual. Astrology is a quick and effective methodology for mapping out the missing pieces and imperfections in our individuation process. By doing so, it can help us lead a more fulfilling and joyful life, where our talents can be highlighted. This is the practical use of astrology, and the most important way to utilize this ancient science.

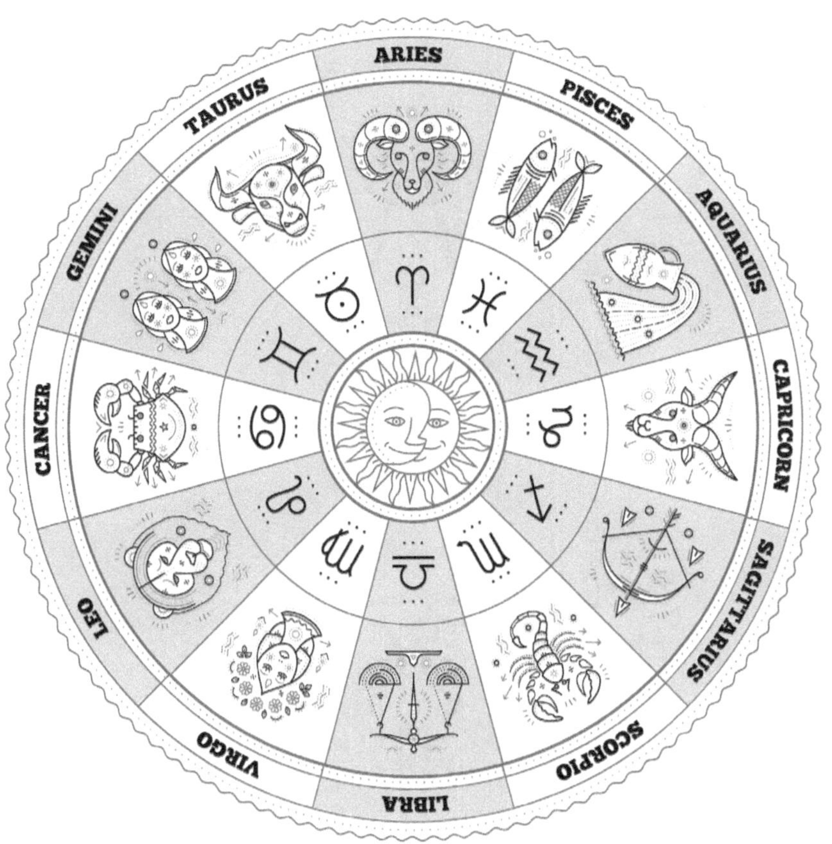

ARIES
TAURUS
PISCES
GEMINI
AQUARIUS
CANCER
CAPRICORN
LEO
SAGITTARIUS
VIRGO
SCORPIO
LIBRA

Aries – Libra axis

For those born under Aries (March 21 - April 19)
or Libra (September 23 - October 22)

The Aries-Libra axis represents the balance between the self and the other. Aries represents the self, independence, and assertiveness, while Libra represents relationships, harmony, and diplomacy. The Aries-Libra axis is also about the relationship between action and consequence. The Aries-Libra axis is fundamentally concerned with fostering social synergy, a delicate balance between individual freedom and the collective need for harmony and productivity.

Famous people born under Aries:
Lady Gaga - March 28, 1986
Robert Downey Jr. - April 4, 1965
Elton John - March 25, 1947
Marlon Brando - April 3, 1924
Emma Watson - April 15, 1990
Mariah Carey - March 27, 1970
Diana Ross - March 26, 1944
Jackie Chan - April 7, 1954
Russell Crowe - April 7, 1964
Sarah Jessica Parker - March 25, 1965

Famous people born under Libra:
Kim Kardashian - October 21, 1980
Hugh Jackman - October 12, 1968
Cardi B - October 11, 1992
Mahatma Gandhi - October 2, 1869
Serena Williams - September 26, 1981
Will Smith - September 25, 1968
Alicia Vikander - October 3, 1988
Martin Heidegger - September 26, 1889
Guillermo del Toro - October 9, 1964
John Lennon - October 9, 1940

ARIES

As an Aries you can improve your life substantially by integrating these Libra qualities:

- **Diplomacy**: Aries can benefit from incorporating more diplomacy into their interactions with others, as opposed to always being direct and forceful.
- **Cooperation**: Aries tend to be independent and self-reliant, but incorporating more cooperation and collaboration can lead to greater success in personal and professional relationships.
- **Fairness**: Libra is known for their sense of fairness and justice, and Aries can benefit from adopting this quality in their own decision-making processes.
- **Compromise**: Aries can have a tendency to be stubborn and inflexible, but practicing the art of compromise can lead to more successful outcomes in conflicts and negotiations.
- **Balance**: Libra is the sign of balance, and incorporating this quality can help Aries avoid burnout and find greater overall equilibrium in their lives.
- **Social graces**: Aries can sometimes come across as brash or abrasive, but incorporating more social graces and etiquette can help smooth out these rough edges.
- **Partnership**: Aries can learn from Libra's emphasis on partnerships and relationships, and benefit from focusing on building and maintaining meaningful connections with others. While individual freedom and development are essential to Aries' nature, relationships and the responsibilities that come with them can be intimidating. Nevertheless, cultivating positive relationships with others can significantly contribute to Aries' personal growth and expand their possibilities.

LIBRA

As a Libra you can improve your life substantially by integrating these Aries qualities:

- **Assertiveness and initiative**: Aries are known for their assertiveness and decisiveness. They are also proactive and take the initiative in pursuing their goals, and Libra can benefit from adopting this same sense of drive and ambition in order to achieve greater success in their personal and professional life.
- **Confidence**: Aries have a strong sense of self-confidence that can be inspiring for Libra, who may struggle with indecision or self-doubt at times.
- **Independence**: Aries are highly independent and self-sufficient, which can be a helpful quality for Libra to adopt in order to avoid becoming overly reliant on others.
- **Courage**: Aries are not afraid to take risks or face challenges head-on, and Libra can benefit from adopting this same sense of courage and bravery in their own life.
- **Passion**: Aries are known for their intense passion and enthusiasm, and incorporating more of this quality can help Libra pursue their goals with greater fervor.
- **Self-assertion**: Aries are not afraid to speak their mind and stand up for what they believe in, and Libra can benefit from developing this same assertiveness and willingness to advocate for themselves.
- **Individual needs**: Aries can demonstrate the courage to end relationships that no longer serve the personal growth and freedom of both partners. On the other hand, Libra's innate desire for harmony can sometimes backfire when the relationship no longer has a vital foundation. It is important for Libras to recognize when a relationship is hindering their individual growth and make the tough decision to move on, even if it means disrupting the peace.

UNDERSTANDING ARIES & LIBRA

When someone asks me if I believe in reincarnation, I can confidently say that it has actually become impossible for me *not* to assume its existence. As an astrologer, I am obviously very familiar with the Lunar Nodes axis. Many Western astrologers have come to the conclusion that the South Lunar Nodes contain a residue of previous incarnations, while the North Lunar Nodes indicate the direction of the present incarnation. A balancing effect constantly occurs between the two.

Interestingly, despite statistical logic, over 60% of my clients for whom I have done manual horoscope readings over the past three decades had the South Lunar Node in Aries and/or the corresponding first house and the North Lunar Node in Libra and/or the corresponding seventh house. This indicates that the Libra-Ram axis is the most problematic in terms of the positions of the Lunar Nodes throughout the zodiac. In essence, the deepest drama in our souls always unfolds in large part through the Lunar Node axis, and negative traits and manifestations of one sign are balanced by the positive ones of the other sign, in all 24 possible variations.

Negative traits of Aries are selfishness, rudeness, violence and cowardice in dealing with one's emotions. Positive traits are courage, pioneering spirit, freedom and a positive sense of self in the face of outside pressure.

Horoscopes that feature a South Node in Libra and a North Node in Aries can be slightly problematic and occasionally troublesome. Individuals with this placement tend to disregard their own needs too much in order to please others. This approach leads to the accumulation of a lot of hidden frustrations and wil manifest itself inevitable in many negative ways such as sarcasm and in rare cases even sadism. It will be clear in this context that Aries can keep Libra balanced, vital and on track as much as Libra can balance Aries.

The Libra-Aries axis essentially revolves around the concepts of "I" and "you", "mine" and "yours", "us" and "them". Libra emphasizes partnership, cooperation, and sharing, while Aries represents the individual's first spark of life and a self-preservation instinct, identity development, and a need for freedom. Aries' raw energy undergoes a process of cultivation, always with an undercurrent of the desire to take charge of something. On the other hand, Libra represents civilized energy that compels one to relinquish a part of oneself in a process of consciousness growth. This is a process in which individuals attempt to transcend their own self and limitations, in order to expand their being and encompass more. One of the ways in which this process occurs is through entering into a relationship.

Alternative opportunities can be found through collaborations. Many people falsely believe that Libra is a superior zodiac sign to Aries, due to its more "civilized image". However, all signs have both positive and negative traits, and none are inherently good or bad.

Systems throughout history, whether they are religious, economic, or political, have interfered with the natural process of self-discovery that exists in every individual. This interference has caused extensive human suffering, revolutions, and wars, regardless of the justifications used. Missionaries and corporations have for example attempted to "civilize" Third World countries (a negative trait associated with Libra) by imposing Western values on unique cultures and people without regard for their distinct characteristics, leading to conflicts and violence (a negative trait associated with Aries) that still persist over a century later.

In contrast to the later stigma of Mars, in ancient Greece, both Venus (the ruler of Libra) and Mars (the ruler of Aries) were seen as protectors of harmony and were included among the *Harmozontai* class of gods (harmony bringers), demonstrating an enlightened concept of reality that is often absent in modern relations and organisations. This idea has also not been fully grasped or adopted by contemporary spirituality.

In a long-term relationship, it's important to strike a balance between sharing and sacrificing for the greater good (Libra), while also allowing space for individual growth and self-discovery (Aries). The healthiest relationships are those in which partners consciously encourage and support each other's personal development. To achieve balance, it's essential to integrate both Venusian and Martian energies in equal measure. However, in Western culture, the planet Mars is often associated only with war and aggression, overlooking its holistic role and undervaluing its qualities such as courage and fearless confrontation. Embracing these Mars-qualities is crucial for genuine spiritual growth.

A similar fate befell Saturn, which, along with Mars, was once labeled as *malefic* or negative, while Venus and Jupiter were considered as *benefics* or positive planets. However, this misunderstanding of Mars and Saturn did not arise in antiquity but in the narrow-minded Christian dogmas of the Middle Ages, and this misconception persists today. Despite the challenges of reconciling the polarities of Libra and Aries in one's personal horoscope, these same difficulties manifest socially. We have witnessed for decades the advance of a mediacratic repressive system in the neo-liberal New World Order process, facilitated by the so-called polder model, a typically negative Libra phenomenon that structurally eradicates the frank and direct, i.e. positive Mars/Aries energy. In response, we have also seen hundreds of thousands of citizens across political, national, and international levels protesting for their individual freedoms. Unfortunately, these two zodiac forces have yet to be effectively and intelligently managed.

Empedocles, a Greek philosopher, developed a significant philosophical concept that revolved around what was later perceived as the apparent conflict between Mars, the ruler of Aries, and Venus, the ruler of Libra. The key idea was that the cooperation of the forces of *strife* (Neikos; Mars) and *love* (Philia; Venus) made life possible. If only strife ruled, life was impossible, and if only love ruled, life was impossible too. Therefore, it was necessary to maintain a dynamic harmony between the principles of separation/differentiation and love/connection. Death occurred when either principle became dominant. This truth is evident to anyone who has a happy marriage, good relationship, or partnership since supporting and nurturing one another without smothering is essential for fruitful interaction.

The Aries-Libra axis is particularly problematic due to the fact that Aries also represents the "mine" while Libra represents the "thine". This creates a natural tension between the self and others, which is inherent in more complex life forms such as humans. On a deeper esoteric level, Aries represents the spark and will of life while Libra represents the symbolic "death" of the personal self and the birth of true connection.

The sign of Libra originally symbolized the setting Sun. In Aries, the energy and influence of the Sun are increased, particularly in the 19th degree of Aries. In contrast, the Sun is at its weakest in Libra, particularly in the 19th degree of Libra where it is said to be in its fall. Sun is also passing *Via Combusta* (the Burnt Way). This runs from 15 Libra to 15 Scorpio as a zone where Sun and Moon have the least influence and Mars and Saturn have the most.

The Sun represents our core identity, making it a challenging task to bring Aries and Libra into synergy. False spiritual systems that equate ego with selfishness further complicate matters. Additionally, the trend of "grab what you can still grab" under constant threat of crises does not help the emancipation of these two zodiac signs.

Philosophically, the contrast between Libra and Aries is elaborated in the life's work of Karl Marx and Max Stirner's book *Der Einzige und sein Eigentum*. Although they had Sun in Taurus and Scorpio respectively, their work interprets the Libra-Aries polarity to an extreme extent.

Balancing the give-and-take in a relationship or cooperation shouldn't be a daunting task. By doing so reasonably and understanding why it's essential for success, you can go a long way. The same applies to creating an ideal society that blends civilization with personal space for individuation, allowing individuals' core qualities to flourish without stifling them for economic gain or political interests. The relationship between culture and wilderness must be balanced, preventing it from tipping to the wrong side as it currently is. Instead of operating in polarity, Libra and Aries must synergize in a nurturing correlation to achieve this balance.

SUMMARY OF THE POSITIVE QUALITIES OF ARIES & LIBRA

ARIES

Aries is the first sign of the zodiac, and it is represented by Aries, reflecting the sign's emphasis on assertiveness and courage. On a mundane level Aries rules over new beginnings, leadership, entrepreneurship, innovation, personal development, sports, the military, construction, metalworking, and mechanics. Here are 10 positive traits, qualities and characteristics of the sign Aries:

1. **Leadership**: Aries are natural leaders who are confident, assertive, and not afraid to take risks. They have a strong desire to be in charge and are often successful in positions of power.

2. **Courage**: Aries are known for their courage and fearlessness. They are not afraid to stand up for what they believe in and are often willing to take on challenges and confrontations.

3. **Independence**: Aries value their independence and freedom, both in their personal and professional lives. They have a strong sense of individuality and are not afraid to go against the status quo.

4. **Energy**: Aries are known for their high energy and enthusiasm. They approach life with passion and vigor and are always on the go.

5. **Pioneering**: Aries are often creative and innovative, with a talent for thinking outside the box. They have a natural ability to come up with new ideas and solutions to problems. These talents combined with their courage provide them with a pioneering nature. Many great discoverers have been motivated by this zodiac sign.

6. **Spontaneity**: Aries enjoy living in the moment and often thrive on spontaneity. They are impulsive and adventurous, always looking for new experiences and opportunities.

7. **Honesty**: Aries are known for their honesty and directness. They value truth and integrity and are not afraid to speak their minds.

8. **Optimism**: Aries have a positive outlook on life and tend to see the best in people and situations. They are optimistic and hopeful, even in the face of adversity.

9. **Passion**: Aries are passionate and intense, both in their personal and professional lives. They approach everything they do with a sense of passion and excitement.

10. **Loyalty**: Aries can be fiercely loyal to their loved ones and are willing to go to great lengths to protect and support them. They value loyalty and expect it in return.

LIBRA

Libra is the seventh astrological sign in the Zodiac, and it is represented by a scale, reflecting the sign's emphasis on balance and harmony. On a mundane level Libra rules over diplomacy, relationships, beauty, aesthetics, law, justice, counseling, design, fashion, luxury items, and fine arts. Here are 10 positive traits, qualities, and features associated with the zodiac sign Libra:

1. **Diplomacy**: Libras are known for their ability to mediate and negotiate, making them excellent diplomats and peacemakers. They have a natural talent for understanding both sides of a situation and finding common ground.

2. **Charm**: Libras are often described as charming, attractive, and charismatic. They have a way of putting others at ease and making them feel comfortable in their presence.

3. **Social skills**: Libras enjoy being around people and are skilled at making friends. They are great conversationalists and know how to make others feel heard and valued.

4. **Fairness**: As the sign of balance and justice, Libras have a strong sense of fairness and strive to treat everyone equally. They are often advocates for social justice and equality.

5. **Creativity and esthetics**: Libras are known for their creativity and

artistic talent. They have an eye for beauty and are often drawn to the arts, including music, dance, and visual arts.

6. **Intelligence**: Libras are intelligent and analytical, with a keen ability to observe and analyze situations. They are often good at problem-solving and finding innovative solutions.

7. **Collaboration**: Libras thrive in collaborative environments and enjoy working with others to achieve a common goal. They are team players and excel in group settings.

8. **Graciousness**: Libras are known for their graciousness and good manners. They have a natural sense of etiquette and know how to conduct themselves in social situations.

9. **Harmony**: Libras value harmony and strive to create balance in all areas of their lives. They are often drawn to peaceful environments and seek to avoid conflict.

10. **Romance**: Libras are often romantic and love being in love. They are sensitive and affectionate partners, and they value emotional connection in their relationships.

SUMMARY OF THE NEGATIVE QUALITIES OF ARIES & LIBRA

ARIES

1. **Impatient**: Aries can be very impatient, especially when they want something or when things aren't moving fast enough for them.

2. **Impulsive**: Aries can be impulsive and may act before thinking things through carefully. This can sometimes lead to poor decision-making.

3. **Aggressive and provocative**: Aries can be aggressive and confrontational, especially when they feel challenged or provoked. They can also get very provocative themselves.

4. **Self-centered**: Aries can be self-centered and may have a tendency to prioritize their own needs and desires over those of others.

The lower developed Aries-types can be very egoistic and rude in their actions, not giving a damn thing about someone else.

5. **Stubborn**: Aries can be stubborn and may be unwilling to change their mind or compromise on issues that are important to them.

6. **Arrogant**: Aries can be arrogant and may believe that they are always right. They may have difficulty accepting feedback or criticism from others.

7. **Fear of emotions**: Aries can be very courageous, but also very afraid to confront themselves with the reality of emotions and feelings. They may be inclined to avoid certain emotional confrontations.

8. **Dishonest**: The lower developed Aries-types may become overly fixated on achieving their goals or winning competitions, even if it requires resorting to dishonest tactics.

9. **Lack of focus**: Aries can have a lack of focus and may struggle to follow through on long-term projects or goals.

10. **Argumentative**: Aries can be argumentative and may enjoy debating or arguing with others. They may sometimes become overly aggressive or defensive in these situations.

LIBRA

1. **Indecisive**: Libra can be indecisive and may struggle with making choices or decisions, especially when there are multiple options.

2. **People-pleasing**: Libra can be people-pleasing and may have a tendency to prioritize the needs and wants of others over their own, thus accumulating a lot of frustrations, that will later emerge in distorted form.

3. **Superficial**: Libra can be superficial and may prioritize appearance and social status over deeper values or qualities.

4. **Manipulative**: Libras are skilled at leveraging their expertise to persuade others and gain support for their goals. They possess a natural charm that allows them to win people over and effectively communicate their ideas. If they encounter opposition, they are

adept at influencing and convincing others to see things from their perspective and can be masters in manipulation.

5. **Avoidant or unreliable**: Libra can be avoidant and may shy away from conflict, confrontation or difficult conversations. This trait can also make them unreliable in the face of: *When the going gets tough the tough get...*

6. **Self-indulgent**: Libras are firm believers in enjoying life's finer things, constantly seeking out pleasure and prioritizing their own happiness. Despite having a charitable nature and a desire to assist others, they can occasionally behave selfishly. Their pursuit of pleasure may lead to them appearing self-centered, disregarding the feelings of those around them and placing their own needs above all else.

7. **Non-confrontational**: Libra can be non-confrontational and may struggle with asserting themselves or standing up for what they believe in.

8. **Inconsistent**: Libra can be inconsistent and may have a tendency to change their mind or direction frequently. Libras tend to be enthusiastic during the planning stage of a project, but they may lose momentum and begin to slack off when it comes time for execution. They may try to find an easy way out rather than confronting problems head-on, which can lead to incomplete tasks.

9. **Codependent**: Libra can be codependent and may have a tendency to rely heavily on others for validation and support.

10. **Self-doubting**: Libras may struggle with self-doubt, leading them to lack confidence in their own judgment and have difficulty expressing their emotions and needs directly. This frustration can sometimes result in passive-aggressive behavior towards others.

Taurus – Scorpio axis

*For those born under Taurus (April 20 - May 20)
or Scorpio (October 23 - November 21)*

The Taurus-Scorpio axis represents a delicate balance between *stability* and *transformation*. Taurus is associated with stability, material comfort, and sensuality, while Scorpio embodies transformation, emotional intensity, and depth. While Taurus represents the capacity to *create something out of nothing*, Scorpio ensures that what is created is seen through to *completion*. Together, they form a powerful polarity that highlights the importance of both holding onto what is reliable and comfortable, as well as the need for change and growth.

Famous people born under Taurus:
Adele - May 5, 1988
Dwayne "The Rock" Johnson - May 2, 1972
George Clooney - May 6, 1961
Queen Elizabeth II - April 21, 1926
Uma Thurman - April 29, 1970
Dennis Hopper - May 17, 1937
William Shakespeare - April 23, 1564
Stevie Wonder - May 13, 1950
Penélope Cruz - April 28, 1974
Mark Zuckerberg - May 14, 1984

Famous people born under Scorpio:
Danny DeVito - November 17, 1944
Ryan Gosling - November 12, 1980
Julia Roberts - October 28, 1967
Steve Zahn - November 13, 1967
Bill Gates - October 28, 1955
Katy Perry - October 25, 1984
Pablo Picasso - October 25, 1881
Emma Stone - November 6, 1988
Owen Wilson - November 18, 1968
Björk - November 21, 1965

TAURUS

As a Taurus you can improve your life substantially by integrating these Scorpio qualities:

- **Intensity**: Scorpio is known for their intense and passionate nature, and Taurus can benefit from incorporating more of this quality into their own pursuits and relationships.
- **Depth**: Scorpio is often associated with depth and complexity, and Taurus can benefit from adopting this same sense of depth in their own thinking and emotional experiences.
- **Cutting the dead wood**: Scorpio is widely recognized for its exceptional capacity to release things that are no longer beneficial. Similarly, Taurus can significantly enhance their creativity and free up mental space by discarding emotional clutter and other factors that drain their energy. By letting go of unnecessary baggage, Taurians can enjoy greater freedom and unlock their full potential.
- **Emotional Intelligence**: Scorpio is highly attuned to emotions, both their own and others, and Taurus can benefit from developing greater emotional intelligence and awareness in their personal and professional relationships.
- **Transformation and process**: Scorpio is associated with transformation and rebirth, and Taurus can benefit from embracing change and transformation in their own life in order to experience growth and evolution. Realizing that life is essentially an ongoing process is a very healthy thing for Taurians to keep in mind!
- **Inner Strength**: Scorpio is a sign that is known for their inner strength and resilience, and Taurus can benefit from developing this same sense of inner fortitude in order to overcome challenges and obstacles in their life.
- **Completion**: Scorpio's unwavering perseverance can play a crucial role in supporting Taurus' creative pursuits, by ensuring that they see things through to completion. While Taurians are known for

their diverse interests and the ability to initiate numerous creative projects out of nothing, they may sometimes abandon them prematurely. Scorpio can provide the necessary push to Taurus to finish what they started, enabling them to fully actualize their creative potential. By working together, the qualities of Scorpio and Taurus can achieve remarkable success in their creative endeavors.

SCORPIO

As a Scorpio you can improve your life substantially by integrating these Taurus qualities:

- **Stability**: As the fixed sign of the Earth-Element, Taurus is known for their stability and grounding presence, and Scorpio can benefit from incorporating more of this quality into their own life to create a sense of security and consistency. Taurus is also highly practical and grounded in reality, and Scorpio can benefit from adopting this same sense of practicality in order to make informed decisions and pursue realistic goals.
- **Creative power**: Taurus, being a Venusian sign, can be highly creative and original, creating something in art, literature, philosophy or even politics out of nothing. Scorpios who recognize that their energy is better channeled towards awakening their latent Taurian creative force, rather than being consumed by control or power plays, have the potential to achieve great successes. The celebrated Scorpio-artist, Pablo Picasso, serves as an excellent role model in this regard.
- **Sensuality**: Taurus is often associated with sensuality and pleasure, and Scorpio can benefit from incorporating more of this quality into their own life to experience greater enjoyment and fulfillment.
- **Humor**: Taurians often have a unique sense of humor, which stems from their ability to see the relativity of the drama in the world in correlation with their talent *not* to be moved or impressed by every

mass-hysterical trend that was enforced by the media, commerce and politics. The lighthearted humor and grounded perspective of Taurians can help Scorpions break free from their obsessive thought patterns and find a more balanced approach to life. John Cleese, the Scorpion-comedian from Monty Python, became a master in exemplifying this Taurian perspective with his sharp wit and clever observations.

- **Loyalty**: Taurus is known for their loyalty and devotion, and Scorpio can benefit from embracing this same sense of loyalty in their personal and professional relationships.

- **Objectivity**: Taurus, in contrast to Scorpio, is naturally related to objectivity because this sign is locked in a unique resonance with the world itself and its hidden natural organization. Scorpio is the most subjective of all zodiac signs. Just as Scorpio can teach Taurus how to embrace the subjective experience of life, thus experiencing life more intensely, Taurus can teach Scorpio about the limitations and dangers of sticking to one subjective perception or perspective. Paradoxically, cultivating Taurian objectivity can keep Scorpios on track as beings that love the process itself more than any other zodiac sign.

- **Financial Responsibility**: Taurus is often associated with financial responsibility and stability, and Scorpio can benefit from adopting this same sense of financial savvy and planning in order to achieve greater financial security and stability in their life.

UNDERSTANDING TAURUS & SCORPIO

The Taurus-Scorpio axis may not be the most troublesome, but it certainly is the most intense. This axis is especially challenging to navigate in today's age of dominant Air energy, characterized by its fast-paced, superficial, and non-committal nature. The Scorpio-Taurus axis governs consciousness at its deepest and most primal level, with powerful energies that are both ancient and compelling. For Taurus, these energies manifest as Eros (Creative Power) and Kaza (Will Universe), while for Scorpio, they take the form of Telos/Thanatos (Completion and Meaning) and Kadar (Personal Will). The dominance of the superficial Air Element in our modern digital times can cause frustration for Scorpio and Taurus, as there is no match with this energy.

"Thoroughbred" Scorpions and Taurians seem to be incompatible with each other, making it difficult to achieve a fruitful synergy between the two signs. This is indeed virtually impossible with the not so bright types in this category. The lower Scorpio type is more vain than the worst Leo, announcing at every birthday party that he or she is a Scorpio (so watch out), and in terms of tattoos, the person in question seems like a walking refrigerator door."

Then there is a second Scorpio type. These can be brilliant artists, with, alas, some unstoppable drive towards alcohol or drugs. The Dutch Scorpio singer and painter Herman Brood, who in my opinion, along with Jean-Michel Basquiat, achieved the absolute top in figurative expressionist painting, combined that artistic genius with a continuous self-destruction, ending in suicide. Then there is the ordinary common people type (as is the case with every sign), the obsessive power or control seeker, the freak who works behind the scenes through control systems, watching, following, tracking people, without their victims being aware of it.

Finally, there are higher Scorpio types who distinguish themselves clearly in the group with a penetrating, unmasking sharpness and confronting honesty. This last type produces admirable people who have reached the highest octave of Scorpio energy by integrating the opposite sign Taurus into their being and thereby maximizing Scorpio's potential. These people can manifest themselves in many areas because they have no fear of complexity and have an enormous reservoir of energy, which they manage well. They can be top surgeons, martial arts or qi-gong masters, politicians, writers, artists, advisors, etc. It is a blessing to have them in your circle of friends.

In the end, it applies to both Scorpio and Taurus that "authenticity" and uncompromising "honesty and (self)confrontation willingness" can only be achieved by perfectly integrating the two zodiac forces. Taurus is the creator who can make something out of nothing, Scorpio provides the authenticity and is the completer of that creative process. In this respect, one force is nothing without the other. Without synergy, they paralyze each other. In synergy, iron can be broken with hands. This realization and its consequences determine whether we get a self-made exemplary person with high standards and values, or a notorious jerk - or someone in a process somewhere between the two, because this axis is always intense. The central theme that connects Scorpio and Taurus could be best formulated as: "Don't be fake! Get real! Life is short and worth living!"

Scorpio, the taboo breaker
Some Scorpios have a strong affinity for complexity and the border areas of the human mind, such as transhumanism or (the analysis of) the criminal brain. Scorpio actress Scarlett Johansson perfectly portrayed the role of Lucy in the eponymous film, and Jodie Foster required a lot of emotional "athleticism" in Silence of the Lambs. In addition to the fact that the highly developed Scorpio has no fear of

complexity (in any area), where most people run away screaming (unraveling is a Scorpio thing, no matter how long it takes), there are other forms of courage that this sign has a certain patent on. Being willing to be a taboo breaker (especially when it comes to a useless taboo) with complete disregard for what "they" will think, was creatively manifested in the Netherlands by few as the writer and artist Jan Wolkers and his themes of sex and death. This ability to see through the nonsense of certain social and cultural customs, rules, chicken-without-a-head assumptions, and wanting to shed that noose, merges in Scorpio with their mechanism of information processing.

Both Scorpio and Taurus process information to the core. This is completely different from Air and Fire signs, which primarily pass on information and thus contribute their valuable part to the whole. Scorpio and Taurus have mastery over becoming deeply conscious and gaining control over the information. The difference between Scorpio and Taurus is that with the latter sign, the information is primarily mirrored against a primal objectivity, and with Scorpio, against a primal subjectivity. However, the outcome is the same. The complexity of this information processing process is the cause of Taurus children often being burdened with comments and notes that they are doing well but are too slow at school, and Scorpio children being told to "keep their big mouth shut."

Perhaps the Taurus and Scorpio-axis is best suited for creative endeavors. Creativity does not necessarily have to be limited to traditional creative disciplines such as art, music, or literature (Salvador Dali, Benjamin Britten, Honore de Balzac). Karl Marx was a creative innovator in the political, philosophical, and socio-economic fields. Freud was creative within psychology, while the Australian publisher Duncan Roads *(Nexus)* and the Dutch Sander Compagner

(De Andere Krant) are pioneering in the alternative news circuit. However, creativity can also be practiced on a very small and private scale and still be very nourishing. Learning to create something from scratch is something that Scorpio masters when integrating Taurus. Attention to detail, technique, and completing the creative process is what Taurus can master by integrating Scorpio. If they keep this in mind, both signs will rarely encounter the negative versions of these signs in their path.

Something about the deepest layers of Taurus should not be missing out here Taurus has a peculiar connection to the world itself, and not only symbolically. If something in the (natural) world is about to go terribly wrong, it feels like a personal pain, threat, or harm to a positive person with a strong Taurus placement in the horoscope. Something that is often not felt or imagined by the other zodiac signs. The relationship between Taurus, the world, and the body is so strong and intense that the boundary between the world and the personal existence disappears and is experienced as one organism. Pollution, dying insects, disappearing forests and natural landscapes, the rise of power politics, all literally cause pain in the soul, and something must be done about it. This urge is so strong because of this interweaving. Hence, Taurus is strongly represented among the founders of the great new trend, thought or concept.

The method of information processing for Scorpio has already been described in this article. However, one shadow aspect has been left unmentioned: the tendency to want to penetrate into something as an intrinsic power. Scorpio energy itself has a tendency to penetrate into everything, including crime and things that belong to the seedy side. This makes people with Sun, Moon, ascendant or many planets in this sign more sensitive to this Plutonian force. Wolkers once said in an interview that he was not a writer who could just make something up. He had to have experienced everything he wrote about himself. The subjective exploration of reality reaches nowhere as deeply as in the Scorpio sign. For Taurus, it is crucial to integrate this quality as well. Taurians who neglect this, often degenerate into totally uninteresting figures, newspaper readers and believers, dull, and messed up. Very different from American black anti-racism activist Malcolm-X (Sun, Moon, Mercury in Taurus), who had integrated Scorpio, or rapper Busta Rhymes (Sun and Mercury in Taurus), who very demonstratively ignores the notorious "slowness" (and aversion to complexity) of Taurus in the intro of 60 seconds Assassin, one of the fastest raps ever produced.

SUMMARY OF THE POSITIVE QUALITIES OF TAURUS & SCORPIO

TAURUS

Taurus is the second astrological sign in the Zodiac, and it is represented by the Bull, reflecting the sign's emphasis on determination and strength. On a mundane level Taurus rules over finance, banking, luxury, agriculture, real estate, architecture, fine arts, singing, gourmet food, textiles, and perfume. Here are some of the positive traits, qualities, and features associated with the zodiac sign Taurus:

1. **Dependability**: Taurians are known for their dependability and reliability. Taurians are loyal and devoted to their loved ones. They are fiercely protective of their friends and family and will do anything to keep them safe and happy.
2. **Determination and Perseverance**: Taurians are highly determined. They are not afraid of hard work and are willing to put in the effort to achieve their goals. They have an incredible amount of endurance and perseverance.

3. **Sensuality**: Taurians are sensual beings who enjoy the pleasures of life. They have a love for food, music, nature, art and sex.

4. **Resourceful**: Taurians often have a strong affinity for both the concepts of 'certainty' and 'objectivity', which leads them to be well-read about a wide range of subjects.

5. **Patience**: Taurians are patient and can endure long periods of waiting and persistence. They have a steady and even-keeled temperament, which makes them excellent problem-solvers. However they should always guard against a situation where patience unconsciously leads to inertia.

6. **Creativity**: Taurians of the creative type can as no other sign create something new out of nothing. In society they are often responsible for the foundation and solidification of something completely new, whether this renewal takes place in art, literature, music, architecture, politics, philosophy or social trend.

7. **Practicality**: Taurians are highly practical and down-to-earth. They have a knack for solving problems and finding practical solutions to complex issues. In contrast to Scorpions Taurians usually like to keep things as simple as possible, usually because technology and administrative stuf are not the things they get very passionate about. When Taurians love complexity it is in most cases some philosophical issue, which originates in the mystical Taurian connection to the (real) world itself in contrast to the simulated reality created by politicians and media.

8. **Wealth**: Taurians are usually good with money. Taurians may not necessarily be interested in money and possessions per se. However, they dislike depending on the money and resources of others because it can interfere with their personal autonomy and will.

9. **Appreciation for beauty and nature**: Taurians have a deep appreciation for beauty and aesthetics. They are drawn to art, music, and design and have a talent for creating beautiful things

themselves. Often there is a deep respect for nature and the Earth which can be experienced as the divine itself.

10. **Truth seeking and guarding**: The higher developed Taurians often act as guardians of truth and human values in the same fanatical way as the higher developed Scorpions tend to do. Get real! is a mutual motto, and the higher developed types born under these signs absolutely detest lies, government manipulations and media indoctrination, and are non compromising.

SCORPIO

Scorpio is the eighth astrological sign in the Zodiac, and it is represented by the Scorpion, reflecting the sign's emphasis on intensity and depth. On a mundane level Scorpio rules over power, control, transformation, secrets, psychology, criminology, forensics, surgery, sex, and metaphysics. Here are some of the positive traits, qualities, and features associated with the zodiac sign Scorpio:

1. **Passion**: Scorpios are known to display either extreme reserve or intense passion and emotion. Those of the passionate type approach everything in life with a sense of unwavering dedication and intensity. Although commonly associated with introversion, Scorpios can also exhibit extroverted tendencies.

2. **Loyalty**: Scorpios are fiercely loyal to their loved ones and will do anything to protect and support them. They value loyalty and expect it in return.

3. **Intuition**: Scorpios have a strong intuition and can sense the emotions and intentions of others. They are often able to see beyond the surface and get to the heart of the matter.

4. **Depth**: Scorpios are known for their depth and complexity. They have a rich inner life and are often drawn to the mysterious, occult and enigmatic.

5. **Courage**: Scorpios are brave and not afraid to confront difficult situations. They have a strong sense of determination and are willing to take risks to achieve their goals. If there are subcutaneous tensions in their relationships with others, they are often the first to name it.

6. **Sensitivity**: Scorpios are sensitive and empathetic. They have a deep understanding of the emotions of others and can be very supportive and nurturing.

7. **Independence**: Scorpios value their independence and are not afraid to stand alone. They have a strong sense of self and are not easily swayed by the opinions of others.

8. **Perseverance**: Just like Taurians, Scorpios are highly perseverant and determined. They are not easily deterred by obstacles and are willing to put in the effort to achieve their goals.

9. **Magnetism**: Scorpios have a natural magnetism that draws others to them. They have a charismatic and compelling presence that can be quite captivating. This magnetism is due to the Plutonian influence on those born under this sign, which has a magical and sort of 'binding' effect on people.

10. **Truth seeking and guarding**: The higher developed Scorpio, just like the higher developed Taurus may also act as a guardian of truth and human values. Scorpions can even express this feature even very daring and provocative. As said before: Get real! is a mutual motto, and just like Taurians, the higher developed Scorpio detests lies, government manipulations and media indoctrination, and will expose them.

SUMMARY OF THE NEGATIVE QUALITIES OF TAURUS & SCORPIO

TAURUS

1. **Stubborn**: Taurus can be very stubborn and may resist change, even when it's for their own good.
2. **Possessive**: Taurus can be possessive and may struggle with jealousy or controlling behavior in relationships.
3. **Materialistic**: Taurus can be materialistic and may place too much emphasis on material possessions and wealth and end up as lonely as Citizen Kane.
4. **Self-indulgent**: Taurus can be self-indulgent and may struggle with overeating, overspending, or other forms of excess.
5. **Workaholic**: Taurians are known to be cautious starters, but once they set their sights on a goal, they become an unstoppable force, capable of moving mountains. However, in their obsessive pursuit of results, they may neglect their own health, social relationships, and other aspects of their lives that they "will give their attention after achieving their objectives." While this laser-like focus is impressive, it also carries a hidden risk of isolation, burn-outs or heart failure.
6. **Inert or creature of habit**: Taurus individuals may sometimes exhibit a tendency towards inertia and procrastination, and may find themselves stuck in a "comfort zone" that leads to social disengagement. While they are not necessarily opposed to change or new directions, they can resemble cats and dogs who thrive on the predictability of daily routines. As a result, they may lack the initiative needed to break free from this pattern.
7. **Resentful and irritable**: Taurus can be resentful and may hold grudges or harbor negative feelings towards others for a long time. Taurians may struggle with managing their emotions, which can sometimes manifest unexpectedly as deep depressions or explosive outbursts of anger. These tendencies may be amplified if they are challenged by some authority figure.

8. **Political correctness**: Taurus can get very attached to the comfort zone and betray his/her real nature thoroughly, by merging with the masses' hysteria and mainstream in general.
9. **Overly cautious**: Taurus can be overly cautious and may struggle with taking risks or trying new things.
10. **Inflexible and uncompromising**: Taurus can be inflexible and may struggle with adapting to new situations or ideas. Taurus can therefore also be uncompromising and may struggle with finding common ground with others or making concessions in conflicts.

SCORPIO
1. **Possessive**: Scorpio can be possessive and may struggle with letting go of people or things that they feel attached to.
2. **Jealous**: Scorpio can be jealous and may have a tendency to become overly protective or territorial in relationships.
3. **Secretive**: Scorpio can be secretive and may be hesitant to share their thoughts or feelings with others.
4. **Suspicious**: Scorpio can be suspicious and may have a tendency to doubt the intentions of others.
5. **Vengeful**: Scorpio can be vengeful and may hold grudges or seek revenge when they feel wronged.
6. **Controlling**: Scorpio can be controlling and may have a tendency to try to manipulate situations or people to get what they want. Scorpio Bill Gates even managed to spread his control mania across the entire planet.
7. **Intense**: Scorpio can be intense and may have a tendency to come on too strong in relationships or interactions.
8. **Obsessive**: Scorpio can be obsessive and may have a tendency to fixate on certain people or things.
9. **Politically correct**: Scorpio like Taurus can betray itself completely by changing truth with political correctness.
   In contrast to Taurians, who do so because they often hate

confrontation and love the comfort zone, Scorpions of this caliber are usually driven by a lust for power or recognition.

10. **Distrustful**: Scorpio can be distrustful and may have a hard time trusting others, especially if they have been betrayed or hurt in the past.

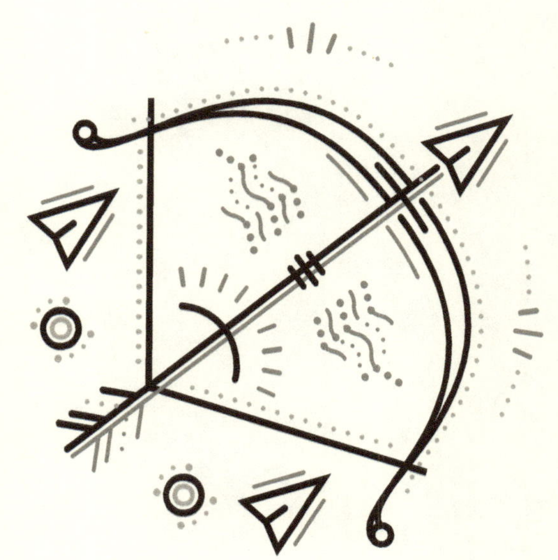

Gemini – Sagittarius axis

For those born under Gemini (May 21 - June 20)
or Sagittarius (November 22 - December 21)

The axis between Gemini and Sagittarius represents the balance between *knowledge* and *wisdom*. Gemini represents the acquisition and sharing of knowledge, communication, and curiosity, while Sagittarius represents higher learning, wisdom, and spirituality. Gemini and Sagittarius can complement each other well, with Sagittarius bringing depth, truth, and focus to Gemini's knowledge-seeking tendencies, and Gemini helping Sagittarius to remain open-minded and avoid academic isolation.

Famous people born under Gemini:

Marilyn Monroe - June 1, 1926
Kanye West - June 8, 1977
Angelina Jolie - June 4, 1975
Johnny Depp - June 9, 1963
Natalie Portman - June 9, 1981
Bob Dylan - May 24, 1941
Morgan Freeman - June 1, 1937
Prince - June 7, 1958
Neil Patrick Harris - June 15, 1973
Venus Williams - June 17, 1980

Famous people born under Sagittarius:

Taylor Swift - December 13, 1989
Brad Pitt - December 18, 1963
Winston Churchill - November 30, 1874
Jay-Z - December 4, 1969
Walt Disney - December 5, 1901
Britney Spears - December 2, 1981
Nicki Minaj - December 8, 1982
Frank Sinatra - December 12, 1915
Jake Gyllenhaal - December 19, 1980
Steven Spielberg - December 18, 1946

GEMINI

As a Gemini you can improve your life substantially by integrating these Sagittarius qualities:

- **Optimism**: Sagittarius is known for their optimistic and adventurous nature, and Gemini can benefit from incorporating more of this positive outlook into their own life.
- **Nature**: The nature-loving Sagittarius contrasts with the urban-focused Gemini. Exploring the great outdoors and taking leisurely strolls can be both enriching and eye-opening, especially compared to Gemini's constant noise and screen time of city living. Nature offers a more peaceful environment, allowing information to sink into the emotional and intuitive layers of the soul, thus leading to a heightened awareness and understanding of the perceived information.
- **Honesty**: Sagittarius is known for their honesty and bluntness, and Gemini can benefit from adopting this same sense of transparency and authenticity in their own communication and relationships.
- **Adventure**: Sagittarius is often associated with adventure and risk-taking, and Gemini can benefit from incorporating more of this sense of adventure and excitement into their own life.
- **Independence**: Sagittarius is highly independent and self-reliant, and Gemini can benefit from adopting this same sense of independence and self-sufficiency in order to pursue their own interests and goals.
- **Focus and purpose**: Gemini's curious and restless mind can sometimes get sidetracked with new and trendy information, potentially missing out on important knowledge. Sagittarius, with their focus and purposeful nature, can help guide Gemini towards the information that truly matters and help them prioritize their pursuit of knowledge.
- **Love of deeper learning**: Sagittarius is often associated with a love of deeper learning and higher education, and Gemini can benefit

from incorporating this same passion for knowledge and intellectual curiosity into their own life.

SAGITTARIUS

As a Sagittarius you can improve your life substantially by integrating these Gemini qualities:

- **Flexibility**: Gemini is known for their flexibility and adaptability, and Sagittarius can benefit from incorporating more of this quality into their own life in order to navigate change and uncertainty.
- **Communication**: Gemini is highly skilled in communication, and Sagittarius can benefit from adopting this same sense of clarity and effectiveness in their own communication with others.
- **Taking things less seriously**: While Sagittarius individuals tend to be naturally optimistic, it would be beneficial for them to recognize the worth of information that is solely meant for entertainment. This is especially important if they are pursuing a career as a novelist. Though a mutable sign, just like Gemini, Sagittarius can be very focused, thus approaching tunnel vision. Gemini primordially picks up information from every direction and every kind indiscriminately.
- **Versatility**: Gemini is highly versatile and able to adapt to different situations and contexts, and Sagittarius can benefit from adopting this same sense of versatility in order to pursue a wide range of interests and experiences.
- **Playfulness**: Gemini is often associated with a sense of playfulness and lightness, and Sagittarius can benefit from incorporating more of this quality into their own life in order to experience greater joy and fun
- **Social skills**: Gemini is highly social and skilled in interpersonal relationships, and Sagittarius can benefit from developing this same sense of social savvy and ability to connect with others.

• **Curiosity**: Gemini is known for their curiosity and questioning nature, and Sagittarius can benefit from adopting this same sense of curiosity and open-mindedness in order to explore new ideas and experiences. This is particularly true when Sagittarian academics fall into the booby trap of accepting the so-called "scientific consensus," which is actually a contradiction in terms since the essence of true science involves maintaining curiosity and an open-minded approach to investigations.

UNDERSTANDING GEMINI & SAGITTARIUS

When a Gemini refuses to integrate with Sagittarius, they risk wasting their life on shallow conversation, consuming pulp-media and internet content, and using DSM-recognized attention disorders as an excuse for their lack of focus. This can prevent them from developing depth, authenticity, and self-control. Another type of unsuccessful Gemini may be a kleptomaniac, con-artist, spammer or spokesperson for a government or multinational corporation who resorts to stealing or lying in order to compensate for their lack of direction and purpose in life, which is something Sagittarius can help them find.

On the other hand, a Sagittarius who isolates themselves from Gemini can become an academic living in an ivory tower, producing valuable publications that only a few people read. Despite the content's potential to benefit society, the language used can fail to connect with a wider audience. Therefore, Sagittarius needs to learn to communicate their knowledge in a way that resonates with a broad public, while Gemini must strive to gain a deeper sense of purpose and focus. By integrating these qualities, they can both achieve greater fulfillment and impact.

Another type of misguided Sagittarius can be observed in the initially idealistic and reasonable politician who quickly transforms into a power-hungry opportunist, flip-flopping on their beliefs to gain favor. Similarly, this type can emerge in religious leaders with a narcissistic and megalomaniac guru complex. They believe they possess the authority to dictate interpretations of the divine and enforce punishment for noncompliance with their narrow-minded views (or for failing to pay membership dues) within a franchise-like employment agreement. This can happen through a pseudo-spiritual multi-level marketing institution such as the Vatican or Church of

Scientology. I understand this opinion may not be popular, but I couldn't resist expressing it. Thankfully, my Sagittarius friends and acquaintances have a great sense of humor.

Sagittarius is the zodiac sign that values freedom the most. While they love acquiring knowledge from books and the internet, they cannot do without nature and often need to recharge by spending time in it. There is a love-hate relationship with civilization that they secretly harbor.

If deprived of their need for freedom, Sagittarians can resort to heavy drinking. This can become a tricky business, as they are known for their jovial nature, which is contagious and often accompanied by roaring fits of laughter, thanks to the influence of their ruling planet, Jupiter. The Centaur is the symbol of Sagittarius because it represents the balance between the wild and Dionysian, and the civilized and educated aspects of the sign.

Many Sagittarians are interested in sports, either participating in them or following the scores and results on radio or TV. Their sense of purpose is reflected in their goal-oriented nature, which is derived from their ruling planet. They have a unique ability to gather and organize information, which can be attributed to their quest for structure.

Jupiter, the planet traditionally associated with the supreme god of the Romans, has a relationship with rulers. In ancient Babylonia, Jupiter/Saturn aspects were observed to predict the fate of kings. The pyramidal structures Sagittarians create are hierarchical, with a spire at the top. However, the shadow side of Sagittarius is that power can corrupt them, and total power can corrupt them completely.

The positive side of Gemini, which involves staying open to new perspectives and developments, can help Sagittarians avoid being caught between conformity and authenticity. They must maintain their essence of growth and expansion, which are the faculties of their ruling planet, Jupiter. Sagittarians in pyramid structures can be caught in a split, but they must remember to integrate the positive side of Gemini.

According to a statistical study conducted by renowned astrologer Robert Zoller, individuals whose Almutem Figuris, or strongest planet, is Jupiter, tend to have lives marked by difficult conditions that can extinguish optimism in almost everyone. For instance, an acquaintance of mine with this planetary configuration works in a hospital ward treating children with cancer. Despite the overwhelming sadness and difficulty of the work, the intrinsic cheerfulness of Jupiter is a crucial source of support for patients and staff alike. Among all the planets, Jupiter is often associated with qualities such as positivity, expansion, and optimism, and is considered the ultimate yang-planet of the solar system.

Gemini is the sign of the zodiac that ranges from the low end of being gossipy, a Twitter addict, a thief, a pathological liar, or a mainstream journalist to the high end of being highly intelligent, broad-minded, quick-thinking, and a masterful communicator who is a delight to be around. The common traits of both low and high types of Gemini are their keen, curious minds and their ability to maintain many contacts. They also tend to take many short trips and are often commuters. However, Gemini's development can be hindered by its difficulty in being truthful. Being an agile and Air sign, Gemini is primarily a connector and not an initiator. This makes it one of the most challenging signs to take a stance or recognize intrinsic life conditions.

Nature provides a solution to this problem by allowing Gemini to pick up and channel information constantly. Around the age of 50, a true identity and individuality crystallize in that immense pool of processed information. Geminis with Mercury in Taurus reach this stage much earlier, and those with Mercury in Cancer make contact earlier with the credo "feeling makes no mistakes in thinking," accelerating the process.

The matured Gemini has taken a specific standpoint after many trials and errors. Nevertheless, the intrinsic trait of Gemini is viewpoint-less information transmission, which easily mixes up truth, genuineness, falsehood, and illusion. Information is not initially measured by points of view but by other information. As a result, the matured Gemini has a more or less ethereal, not fixed, but very stable point of view, which manifests itself in the ability to put things, people, and situations into perspective. A recognition of the good in nature and humanity shines through between the lines of this perspective. Moreover, this Gemini is no longer afraid of the long road. These qualities are evident in the mainstream journalist who no longer follows the credos of their newspaper or TV editors and becomes one of the better investigative journalists.

SUMMARY OF THE POSITIVE QUALITIES OF GEMINI & SAGITTARIUS

GEMINI

Gemini is the third astrological sign in the Zodiac, and it is represented by the Twins, reflecting the sign's emphasis on duality and versatility. On a mundane level Gemini rules over communication, transportation, commerce, media, journalism, writing, teaching, social media, networking, comedy, short-distance travel, and small electronic devices. Here are some of the positive traits, qualities, and features associated with the zodiac sign Gemini:

1. **Adaptability**: Geminis are highly adaptable and versatile. They are able to adjust to new situations and environments quickly and easily.
2. **Intelligence**: Geminis often are highly intelligent and curious. They have a thirst for knowledge and enjoy learning about a wide range of subjects.
3. **Communication**: Geminis are excellent communicators and have a talent for expressing themselves clearly and persuasively. They are often skilled writers, speakers, and teachers.
4. **Humor**: Geminis have a great sense of humor and love to make others laugh. They have a talent for finding the humor in any situation. "Why so serious?" could be a Gemini motto.
5. **Flexibility**: Geminis are highly flexible and open-minded. They are not set in their ways and are willing to consider new ideas and perspectives.
6. **Sociability**: Geminis are sociable and enjoy being around others. They have a talent for making friends and are often the life of the party.
7. **Curiosity**: Geminis are naturally curious and inquisitive. They have a thirst for knowledge and enjoy exploring new ideas and experiences.

8. **Versatility**: Geminis are highly versatile and adaptable. They are able to handle a wide range of tasks and can excel in many different areas.
9. **Energy**: Geminis are energetic and lively. They have a zest for life and enjoy staying active and engaged in a variety of activities.
10. **Creativity**: Geminis can be creative and imaginative, especially in the field of writing. They have a talent for thinking outside the box and coming up with unique and innovative ideas.

SAGITTARIUS

Sagittarius is the ninth astrological sign in the Zodiac, and it is represented by the Archer, reflecting the sign's emphasis on adventure, exploration, and optimism. On a mundane level Sagittarius rules over exports, long journeys, large transportation, aerospace, higher education, universities, the Vatican, foreign countries, broadcasters, prophets, visions, advertising agencies, horses, the equestrian world, editors, philosophy, and theology. Here are some of the positive traits, qualities, and features associated with the zodiac sign Sagittarius:

1. **Adventurous**: Sagittarians are adventurous and love to explore. They have a thirst for new experiences and may enjoy travel, outdoor activities, or trying new foods and cultures.
2. **Optimistic**: Sagittarians are optimistic and positive. They have a can-do attitude and are able to see the bright side of any situation.
3. **Intellectual**: Sagittarians are intellectual and philosophical. They have a talent for abstract thinking and may be drawn to subjects such as religion, spirituality, or metaphysics.
4. **Independent**: Sagittarians are independent and self-reliant. They value their freedom and may resist being tied down by commitments or obligations.
5. **Humorous**: Sagittarians, especially when having integrated their

unconscious self, Gemini, are often humorous and lighthearted. They enjoy making others laugh and often have a quick wit.

6. **Enthusiastic**: Sagittarians are enthusiastic and passionate. They throw themselves into their interests and hobbies with gusto and energy.

7. **Curious**: Sagittarians are curious and inquisitive. They have a thirst for knowledge and may be interested in a wide variety of subjects.

8. **Open-minded**: Sagittarians are open-minded and accepting of others. They are not judgmental and are willing to listen to different perspectives and ideas.

9. **Generous**: Sagittarians are generous and giving. They may be involved in philanthropic causes or may simply enjoy giving gifts and helping others.

10. **Ethical**: Sagittarians are ethical and principled. They have a strong sense of right and wrong and may be drawn to careers in law, social justice, or activism.

SUMMARY OF THE NEGATIVE QUALITIES OF GEMINI & SAGITTARIUS

GEMINI

1. **Superficial**: Gemini can be superficial and may focus too much on appearances or surface-level qualities.
2. **Inconsistent**: Gemini can be inconsistent and may struggle with following through on commitments or maintaining stable relationships.
3. **Indecisive**: Gemini can be indecisive and may struggle with making important decisions or sticking to a course of action.
4. **Restless**: Gemini can be restless and may struggle with boredom or feeling trapped in one place or situation.
5. **Gossipy**: Gemini can be gossipy and may struggle with keeping confidential information to themselves.
6. **Two-faced**: Gemini can be two-faced and may say different things to different people or present different personas in different situations. They can also be unreliable and may struggle with keeping their promises or showing up on time.
7. **(Social)media addicted**: Of all signs Gemini are the most at risk of getting addicted to (social) media, and thus getting completely detached from real life.
8. **Stealing**: The negative Gemini can get involved in theft, or all kind of fraudulent activity, including cyber-crimes.
9. **Impulsive**: Gemini can be impulsive and may act without thinking things through, which can sometimes lead to poor decision-making.
10. **Anxious**: Gemini can be anxious and may struggle with worry or overthinking, which can lead to stress and anxiety.

SAGITTARIUS

1. **Impatient**: Sagittarius can be impatient and may struggle with waiting for things or people.
2. **Blunt**: Sagittarius can be blunt and may have a tendency to speak their mind without considering the feelings of others.
3. **Insensitive**: Sagittarius can be insensitive and may have a tendency to overlook or downplay the emotions of others. They can also be inconsiderate and may have a tendency to prioritize their own needs and desires over those of others.
4. **Restless**: Sagittarius can be restless and may have a tendency to seek out new experiences or adventures at the expense of stability or consistency.
5. **Arrogant**: Sagittarius can be arrogant and may have a tendency to believe that they are always right.
6. **Irresponsible**: Sagittarius can be irresponsible and may struggle with following through on commitments or obligations.
7. **Inconsistent**: Sagittarius can be inconsistent and may have a tendency to change their mind or direction frequently. Traditionally hypocrisy is also attributed to the negative Sagittarius.
8. **Impulsive**: Sagittarius can be impulsive and may have a tendency to act without thinking through the consequences.
9. **Judgmental**: Sagittarius can be judgmental and may have a tendency to form opinions about people or situations without fully understanding them.
10. **Hypocrite**: Sagittarians, who are often drawn to influential roles in politics, universities, and religious organizations, may face challenges in maintaining consistency between their personal values and professional aspirations. In some cases, a Sagittarius may struggle with the temptation to prioritize their career ambitions over their ethical principles, potentially leading to hypocritical behavior.

Cancer – Capricorn axis

For those born under Cancer (June 21 - July 22) or Capricorn (December 22 - January 19)

The Cancer-Capricorn axis represents a balance between *nurturing* and *structure*. Cancer represents nurturing, emotional connection, and home life, while Capricorn represents structure, responsibility, and career. This axis also connects the needs one has in their *private life* and the duties their *public life* demands. The energy of Capricorn is earthy, fixed, and concept-oriented, while the energy of Cancer is flowing and reactive to subtle energies and emotional reality. Capricorn is governed by Saturn, and Cancer is governed by the Moon.

Famous people born under Cancer:
Princess Diana - July 1, 1961
Tom Hanks - July 9, 1956
Elon Musk - June 28, 1971
Selena Gomez - July 22, 1992
Liv Tyler - July 1, 1977
Meryl Streep - June 22, 1949
Sylvester Stallone - July 6, 1946
Post Malone - July 4, 1995
Lindsay Lohan - July 2, 1986
Harrison Ford - July 13, 1942

Famous people born under Capricorn:
Martin Luther King Jr. - January 15, 1929
Muhammad Ali - January 17, 1942
Kate Middleton - January 9, 1982
Dolly Parton - January 19, 1946
Bradley Cooper - January 5, 1975
Elvis Presley - January 8, 1935
David Bowie - January 8, 1947
Lin-Manuel Miranda - January 16, 1980
Denzel Washington - December 28, 1954
David Lynch - January 20, 1946

CANCER

As a Cancer you can improve your life substantially by integrating these Capricorn qualities:

- **Discipline**: Capricorn is known for their discipline and hardworking nature, and Cancer can benefit from incorporating more of this quality into their own life in order to achieve their goals and aspirations. Cancer can learn from Capricorn to establish healthy boundaries, take on responsibilities, and pursue long-term goals.
- **Responsibility**: Capricorn is highly responsible and reliable, and Cancer can benefit from adopting this same sense of responsibility in their personal and professional life.
- **Organization**: Capricorn is often associated with organization and planning, and Cancer can benefit from incorporating more of this sense of structure and organization into their own life. They can learn to use their nurturing skills to create a stable and supportive home environment, while also pursuing their career ambitions.
- **Ambition**: Capricorn is highly ambitious and driven, and Cancer can benefit from developing this same sense of ambition and determination in order to pursue their own goals and aspirations.
- **Practicality**: Capricorn is known for their practicality and grounded nature, and Cancer can benefit from adopting this same sense of practicality in order to make informed decisions and pursue realistic goals.
- **Patience**: Capricorn is highly patient and persevering, and Cancer can benefit from developing this same sense of patience in order to navigate challenges and overcome obstacles.
- **Long-term planning**: Capricorn is often associated with long-term planning and foresight, and Cancer can benefit from incorporating more of this sense of future-oriented thinking into their own life in order to achieve greater success and stability.

CAPRICORN

As a Capricorn you can improve your life substantially by integrating these Cancer qualities:

- **Emotional Intelligence**: Cancer is known for their emotional intelligence and ability to connect with others on a deep level, and Capricorn can benefit from developing this same sense of emotional awareness in their own relationships.
- **Nurturing**: Cancer is highly nurturing and caring, and Capricorn can benefit from adopting this same sense of compassion and empathy in their personal and professional interactions. Nurturing includes taking care of one's private needs. Cancer can also help Capricorn to recognize and address any tendencies towards overwork or neglect of personal relationships, which can lead to burnout and dissatisfaction.
- **Creativity**: Cancer is often associated with creativity and imagination, and Capricorn can benefit from incorporating more of this sense of innovation and originality into their work and personal projects.
- **Intuition**: Cancer is highly intuitive and able to sense what others are feeling, and Capricorn can benefit from developing this same sense of intuition in order to make better decisions and navigate complex situations.
- **Flexibility**: Cancer can also help Capricorn to recognize and address any tendencies towards rigidity or inflexibility, which can hinder their ability to adapt to changing circumstances. Cancer is often adaptable and able to navigate change, and Capricorn can benefit from incorporating more of this quality in order to remain open to new opportunities and possibilities.
- **Family values**: Cancer is highly family-oriented and values close relationships with loved ones, and Capricorn can benefit from adopting this same sense of family values in their own personal life.

• **Sensitivity**: Cancer is known for their sensitivity and ability to pick up on subtle nuances in their environment, and Capricorn can benefit from developing this same sense of sensitivity in order to better understand the needs of those around them.

UNDERSTANDING CANCER & CAPRICORN

Cancerians are empathetic and emotional beings, which makes them great listeners and friends. They are intuitive and can sense the emotions of others, which makes them excellent at offering emotional support. Cancers are known for being nurturing, and they love to take care of the people they love. They are also known for their loyalty and devotion towards their family and loved ones. Cancerians value their relationships deeply. They tend to be nurturing and supportive in their relationships, and they love to take care of their partner. They however need a partner who can understand and accept their sensitivity. They also tend to be romantic and enjoy creating a cozy and intimate home environment.

Yet, Cancerians are also known for being moody and sensitive. Cancerians tend to struggle with emotional instability and high sensitivity issues as they pick up a lot of "hidden" energetic information from the environment and other people, which can cause them to suddenly become moody in an unpredictable way - seldom understood by others. They also have a tendency to hold on to grudges and can be very defensive. Cancerians can be insecure in relations and need constant reassurance from their loved ones. For emotional reasons they can abruptly withdraw themselves from social situations. Another tendency is towards claiming, especially emotional claiming.

On the plus side Cancer can bestow a high emotional intelligence on the persons born under this sign. Especially when having gained control over their emotional instability by integrating their unconscious self, the Capricorn, Cancerians can develop into hard and persistent workers, and they are very dedicated to their work. Sylvester Stallone's story of persevering despite facial palsy and being rejected literally a thousand times in his job applications is a testament to almost superhuman determination. Similarly, Mike Tyson, known for his knockout punches, challenges the stereotype of oversensitive Cancerians. Those born under this sign tend to careers that involve helping others, such as nursing, social work, teaching, and counseling. Cancerians are also creative and imaginative, which can make them great artists, actors, writers, and musicians. They often love working from home, as they tend to be introverted and prefer a quiet and peaceful environment.

Capricorn and Accountability: A Path to Freedom
To understand Capricorn as raw energy, one must understand its ruler Saturn. Saturn and Capricorn rule over the hard parts of our bodies, hard character traits, coldness, and resilience because Saturn embodies the metaphysical principle of contraction and thus the domain of yin energy, the negative singularity. Saturn represents an elemental energy, namely the contraction principle itself. In the human psyche, contraction translates as fear and wanting to control out of fear and lack of creative courage, thus making it the most difficult energy to control and integrate.

Saturn is usually misunderstood due to its primordial association with fear and control and also with seriousness, the sacred, the gloomy and reverence for status. However, Saturn is not more serious than any other planet and should therefore also be treated as any other planet. Like every bird sings according to its breed, Saturn displays its Saturnal instead of "serious" characteristics.

Understanding Saturn is crucial to manifesting its positive traits, which include providing structure and formation, taking responsibility, perseverance, realism, stability and good time planning. Moreover, the accumulation of experience and expertise is also a positive trait linked to Saturn and Capricorn. Positive Capricorns are reliable, self-sacrificing hard workers, perfectionists, and exhibit excellent logical and technical skills.

Capricorn's metabolism is the most efficient of all zodiac signs. The positive Capricorn has learned to recognize the dark side of their sign and is averse to vacuous ambition. They possess a good sense of humor and are capable of enjoying life. While mistakes can happen, the positive Capricorn understands that proactive attitude is necessary for achieving freedom. If every person on this planet, no matter their past history, pain, or trauma, and no matter the cause or source, were to let go of victim-hood and take full responsibility for their own lives, the world could truly become a better place. The artificial system of simulated reality that currently exists in the world would collapse, giving rise to a natural human system where billions of unique processes emerge. Each individual would strive to flourish in their own unique way, utilizing their talents and reaching their full potential. Existence would slowly move away from "enforced organization & control" towards a state of "organic thrive".

Positive Capricornians are usually disciplined and focused individuals who are driven to achieve their goals. They are ambitious and hardworking, down to earth types, and they have a strong sense of responsibility towards themselves and others. Capricorns are known for their practicality and their ability to make experience based and pragmatic decisions. They are also patient and persistent, and they don't give up easily.

Career and Work are very important. Capricornians are dedicated individuals who set high goals for themselves. They are driven, disciplined and focused, and they have a strong sense of responsibility towards their work, which makes them great at managing projects and teams. Capricorns excel in careers, such as business, finance, administrating and law, thanks to their organizational and managerial abilities. They make excellent leaders. Politics can also appeal to them, especially when their urge to control is dominant.

In relation to others Capricorns can be too reserved and serious, and they tend to keep their emotions to themselves. They are not very expressive, and they can come across as cold or distant. Capricorns are also known for being cautious and conservative, and they tend to be risk-averse. On an emotional level, Capricorns should regularly indulge in self-care and avoid bottling up emotions. Capricorns value stability and security in their relationships, and they tend to be committed and loyal partners. Being practical and pragmatic, they tend to approach their relationships in a practical way, which may challenge them in the field of emotions and self expression. They can also struggle with perfectionism, and they may have high standards for themselves and others. On the plus side, there are a lot of Capricornians that take their own seriousness with a grain of salt and express a good sense of humor, which highly elevates their personality.

Cancer and Capricorn dichotomy
Cancer is known as the sign of the ordinary people, while Capricorn is known as the sign of rulers and governments. This dichotomy arises from the fact that Cancer represents the private, personal life, while Capricorn represents the public, professional life.
Cancer is associated with home, family, and personal life. Individuals born under this sign are nurturing, empathetic, and emotional.

They value their relationships with loved ones and enjoy creating a cozy, intimate home environment. Cancerians tend to prioritize their personal needs and those of their family over their professional duties. Capricorn, on the other hand, is associated with career, public life, and government. They value their professional status and tend to prioritize their duties towards their job and the larger society over their personal needs.

The dichotomy between Cancer and Capricorn thus arises from the tension between the private and public spheres of life. Individuals born under Cancer tend to prioritize their personal needs and those of their loved ones. They value emotional support and nurturing relationships, which they find in their family and home environment. Cancerians are usually content with a simple life that allows them to focus on their personal needs. Capricornians, on the other hand, tend to prioritize their professional duties and responsibilities. They value their position in society and tend to be ambitious in their career. Capricornians are focused on achieving their goals and tend to sacrifice their personal needs to meet their professional obligations.

It's important to note that our feelings do not necessarily cloud our thinking and decision-making processes. When we pursue a career that does not align with our true desires and aspirations, we inadvertently become our own obstacles. This path often leads to burnout and dissatisfaction. Cancer emphasizes the significance of nurturing our inner lives and fulfilling our innermost needs, which may not be related to the external world, but bring us immense satisfaction. Ultimately, life loses its essence without feelings.

Capricornian political leaders should prioritize meeting the needs of the people they represent, rather than solely focusing on "higher politics." It's important for them to engage with the public regularly and ensure that their policies and decisions align with the interests of the population. However, citizens should also take an active role in shaping their society and not solely rely on politicians to do so. They can assume responsibility for their lives by staying informed about current events and advocating for issues that matter to them. By taking ownership of their role as citizens, they can help minimize the need for political interventions to correct societal problems.

SUMMARY OF THE POSITIVE QUALITIES OF CANCER & CAPRICORN

CANCER

Cancer is the fourth astrological sign in the Zodiac, and it is represented by the Crab, reflecting the sign's emphasis on emotional sensitivity and protection. On a mundane level Cancer rules over home, family, nurturing, emotional intelligence, psychology, history, archaeology, marine biology, food and beverage, hospitality, and interior design. Here are some of the positive traits, qualities, and features associated with the zodiac sign Cancer:

1. **Emotional intelligence**: Cancerians have a deep understanding of their own emotions and the emotions of others. They are highly empathetic and intuitive, and can often sense the needs and feelings of those around them.
2. **Nurturing**: Cancerians are natural nurturers and caregivers. They have a strong desire to care for and protect those they love, and are often seen as the "mom" or "dad" of their friend group.
3. **Loyalty**: Cancerians are fiercely loyal to those they love. They are dedicated and committed, and will go to great lengths to protect and support their loved ones.

4. **Creativity**: Cancerians are highly creative and imaginative. They have a talent for expressing themselves through art, music, writing, or other forms of creative expression.

5. **Intuition**: Cancerians are highly intuitive and can often sense the feelings and emotions of others before they are even expressed. They have a talent for understanding the unspoken needs of those around them.

6. **Sensitivity**: Cancerians are highly sensitive and emotional. They are deeply affected by the world around them and often have strong reactions to their environment.

7. **Tenacity**: Cancerians are tenacious and determined. They have a strong work ethic and are willing to put in the time and effort to achieve their goals.

8. **Home-oriented**: Cancerians are deeply connected to their homes and families. They value their domestic life and often prioritize their home environment over other aspects of their life.

9. **Adaptability**: Cancerians are adaptable and flexible. They are able to adjust to new situations and environments quickly and easily.

10. **Empathy**: Cancerians have a strong sense of empathy and are able to connect with others on a deep emotional level. They have a talent for understanding the feelings and emotions of others.

CAPRICORN

Capricorn is the tenth astrological sign in the Zodiac, and it is represented by the Mountain Goat, reflecting the sign's emphasis on determination, discipline, and ambition. On a mundane level Capricorn rules over the status quo, consensus, business, management, politics, government, law enforcement, finance, economics, architecture, engineering, and mountain climbing. Here are some of the positive traits, qualities, and features associated with the zodiac sign Capricorn:

1. **Ambitious**: Capricorns are highly ambitious and driven. They have a strong desire to succeed in their chosen career or field, and are willing to work hard to achieve their goals.
2. **Responsible**: Capricorns are responsible and dependable. They take their commitments seriously and are often seen as the "adults" of their friend group.
3. **Practical**: Capricorns are practical and grounded. They have a strong sense of reality and are able to make sound, logical decisions.
4. **Disciplined**: Capricorns are highly disciplined and focused. They have a strong work ethic and are able to stay on task and achieve their goals.
5. **Organized**: Capricorns are highly organized and efficient. They have a talent for planning and are able to manage their time and resources effectively.
6. **Patient**: Capricorns are patient and persistent. They are able to stay the course and work towards their goals, even when progress is slow.
7. **Reliable**: Capricorns are reliable and trustworthy. They take their commitments seriously and can be counted on to follow through on their promises.
8. **Self-disciplined**: Capricorns are highly self-disciplined and self-motivated. They are able to set goals for themselves and work towards them without external motivation.
9. **Strategic**: Capricorns are strategic and forward-thinking. They have a talent for planning and are able to see the big picture when making decisions.
10. **Resourceful**: Capricorns are resourceful and practical problem-solvers. They are able to find creative solutions to challenges and are often seen as "fixers" by their friends and colleagues.

SUMMARY OF THE NEGATIVE QUALITIES OF CANCER & CAPRICORN

CANCER
1. **Moody**: Cancer can be moody and may experience frequent, uncontrolled mood swings or changes in emotions.
2. **Overly sensitive**: Cancer can be overly sensitive and may take things personally or get easily hurt. They may overreact or become misplaced defensive in response to criticism or feedback.
3. **Clingy**: Cancer can be clingy and may struggle with letting go of people or situations that are no longer healthy or beneficial.
4. **Passive-aggressive**: Cancer can be passive-aggressive and may express their negative feelings in indirect or subtle ways.
5. **Possessive**: Cancer can be possessive and may struggle with jealousy or controlling behavior in relationships.
6. **Insecure**: Cancer can be insecure and may struggle with self-doubt or low self-esteem.
7. **Resentful**: Cancer can be resentful and may hold grudges or harbor negative feelings towards others for a long time.
8. **Too introverted**: Cancer can be too introverted, lacking the courage or assertiveness to break away from negative relations or situations.
9. **Avoidant**: Cancer can be avoidant and may struggle with confronting difficult situations or having difficult conversations.
10. **Claiming**: Cancer can tend to emotional blackmail and claiming, thus manifest a form of energy sucking.

CAPRICORN

1. **Pessimistic**: Capricorn can be pessimistic and may have a tendency to focus on the negative aspects of situations or outcomes.
2. **Stubborn**: Capricorn can be stubborn and may have a tendency to hold onto their own opinions or ideas, even in the face of new information or evidence.
3. **Cold**: Capricorn can be cold and may struggle with expressing emotions or connecting with others on an emotional level.
4. **Materialistic**: Capricorn can be materialistic and may have a tendency to place a high value on wealth, status, and possessions.
5. **Controlling**: Capricorn can be controlling and may have a tendency to try to manipulate situations or people to get what they want.
6. **Judgmental**: Capricorn can be judgmental and may have a tendency to form opinions about people or situations without fully understanding them.
7. **Inflexible**: Capricorn can be inflexible and may have a tendency to resist change or new ways of thinking.
8. **Workaholic**: Capricorn can be a workaholic and may have a tendency to prioritize work or career over other aspects of their life, such as relationships or hobbies.
9. **Rigid**: Capricorn can be rigid and may have a tendency to adhere strictly to rules, guidelines, or traditions.
10. **Aloof**: Capricorn can be aloof and may have a tendency to keep others at a distance, even in close relationships.

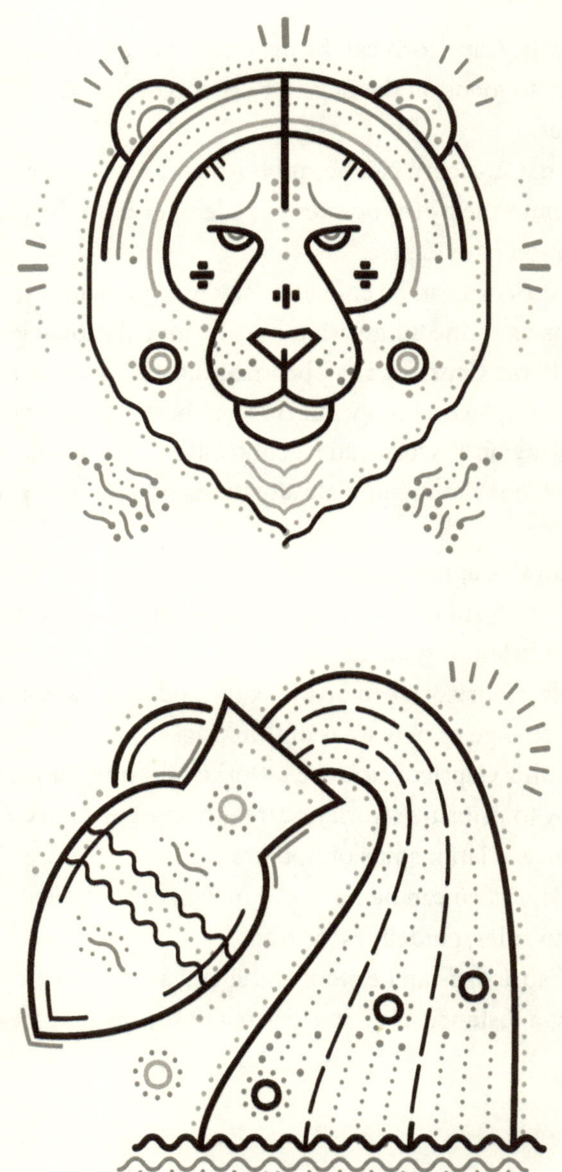

Leo – Aquarius axis

*For those born under Leo (July 23 - August 22)
or Aquarius (January 20 - February 18)*

The Leo-Aquarius axis represents the balance between *self-expression* and *community work*. Leo represents individual creativity, self-expression, and leadership, while Aquarius represents collective consciousness, social change, and humanitarianism. Leo can benefit from Aquarius' emphasis on social responsibility, collaboration, and expanding one's perspective. On the other hand, Aquarius can learn to appreciate Leo's focus on individuality, creativity, and warmth. By exchanging these traits, Leo and Aquarius can broaden their horizons and become more well-rounded individuals.

Famous people born under Leo:
Andy Warhol - August 6, 1928
Madonna - August 16, 1958
Jennifer Lopez - July 24, 1969
Kylie Jenner - August 10, 1997
Daniel Radcliffe - July 23, 1989
Arnold Schwarzenegger - July 30, 1947
Sandra Bullock - July 26, 1964
Mick Jagger - July 26, 1943
Mila Kunis - August 14, 1983
Steve Carell - August 16, 1962

Famous people born under Aquarius:
Oprah Winfrey - January 29, 1954
Ellen DeGeneres - January 26, 1958
Cristiano Ronaldo - February 5, 1985
Bob Marley - February 6, 1945
Jennifer Aniston - February 11, 1969
Justin Timberlake - January 31, 1981
Abraham Lincoln - February 12, 1809
Shakira - February 2, 1977
Michael Jordan - February 17, 1963
Lord Byron -Januari 22, 1788

LEO

As a Leo you can improve your life substantially by integrating these Aquarius qualities:

- **Open-mindedness**: Aquarius is known for their open-mindedness and ability to see things from different perspectives, and Leo can benefit from incorporating more of this quality in order to remain receptive to new ideas and experiences. Aquarius' love of learning and exploration can help Leo become more intellectually curious and expand their knowledge in new and exciting ways.
- **Innovative creativity**: Aquarius is often associated with innovative creativity. Integrating Aquarius' innovative and forward-thinking qualities can help Leo become more innovative in their own pursuits and come up with new and exciting ideas.
- **Independent thinking**: Aquarius is highly independent and values individuality, and Leo can benefit from adopting this same sense of independent thinking in order to make decisions that are aligned with their own values and beliefs.
- **Humanitarianism**: Aquarius is often associated with a strong sense of social justice and humanitarianism, and Leo can benefit from incorporating more of this sense of concern for the greater good into their own life.
- **Non-conformity**: Aquarius is often non-conformist and unafraid to be different, and Leo can benefit from developing this same sense of individuality and not being afraid to stand out.
- **Greater focus on the community**: Leo can benefit from integrating Aquarius' community-oriented qualities, which can help them become more involved in social causes and give back to their community.
- **Visionary thinking**: Aquarius is often associated with visionary thinking and a sense of foresight, and Leo can benefit from adopting this same sense of future-oriented thinking in order to pursue their own long-term goals and aspirations.

AQUARIUS

As an Aquarius you can improve your life substantially by integrating these Leo qualities:

- **Confidence in self expression**: Leo is known for their confidence and self-assuredness, and Aquarius can benefit from developing this same sense of self-confidence in order to pursue their goals and aspirations. Aquarius can also benefit from integrating Leo's expressive qualities, which can help them become more confident in expressing themselves and sharing their ideas with others.
- **Creativity**: Leo is often associated with creativity and artistic expression, and Aquarius can benefit from incorporating more of this sense of originality, creativity and a greater appreciation for the arts into their own life. Leo's love of the arts can help Aquarius develop a greater appreciation for music, theater, and other forms of creative expression.
- **Leadership**: Leo is often a natural leader and takes charge of situations, and Aquarius can benefit from adopting this same sense of leadership in order to achieve their goals and make a positive impact.
- **Passion and playfulness**: Leo is highly passionate and driven, and Aquarius can benefit from developing this same sense of passion and enthusiasm in order to pursue their own interests and goals. Leo's fun-loving and playful nature can help Aquarius become more lighthearted and enjoy life more fully.
- **Generosity**: Leo is known for their generosity and willingness to give to others, and Aquarius can benefit from adopting this same sense of generosity in their personal relationships and community involvement.
- **Charm**: Leo is often charming and charismatic, and Aquarius can benefit from developing this same sense of charm in order to better connect with others and build relationships.

- **Courage**: Leo is often brave and unafraid to take risks, and Aquarius can benefit from developing this same sense of courage in order to pursue their own goals and stand up for their beliefs.

UNDERSTANDING LEO & AQUARIUS

There is an interesting explanation for the eccentricity of Aquarius and centralism of Leo. Uranus, the ruler of Aquarius, has a distinct rotational axis that is roughly perpendicular to the axis of all the other planets. This astrophysical characteristic reflects the unconventional, innovative, and even rebellious nature of Aquarius. People born under this sign often exhibit a free-spirited and independent personality, and they are not afraid to challenge traditional beliefs and norms.

On the other hand, Leo is ruled by the Sun, which is at the center of our solar system. The Sun is the gravitational force that holds all the planets in orbit, and its radiant energy provides life and vitality to our planet. The fixed nature of the Sun's position in Leo reflects the strong sense of self and leadership qualities that are often associated with this sign. People born under Leo are known for their confidence, charisma, and ability to command attention. The sign Leo differs from all other signs in that the sign ruler (Sun) is ALWAYS in the same sign, which is of course Leo! So if you are a Leo you also always have your ruler in Sun-sign. That is unique. An Aries for example can have its ruler Mars in any of the 12 signs, Taurus, ruled by Venus always has its ruler in Aquarius, Pisces, Aries, Taurus, Gemini, Cancer or Leo as Venus never moves further than 72 degrees from the sun. This unique situation of Leos makes them naturally strong and self assured personalities. On the negative side it does not help with self reflection and can hinder self development.

The ruling planet plays a significant role in a person's horoscope, influencing their personality and traits. When the ruling planet is in a sign other than the Sun sign, it can enhance self-awareness by allowing the person to view their own functioning and being from the perspective of that sign's energy and psychosphere. However, Leo individuals may lack this reflective effect because their ruling planet, the Sun, is always in their own sign, creating a potential blind spot and inherent self-absorption. Fortunately, the cosmos has accounted for this by making all planets segments of the essence of the Sun itself, akin to how the colors of the spectrum are facets of white light.

Those born under the sign of Leo are therefore known for their natural leading abilities. They are confident, ambitious, and have a strong sense of self-worth. They are not afraid to take risks and are not afraid to fail. They are also creative, imaginative, and have a flair for the dramatic. Leos are passionate and enthusiastic individuals. They have a zest for life and are always looking for new experiences. They are also generous and warm-hearted, and they love to share their good fortune with others. Leos are natural entertainers and love to be the center of attention.

On the other hand, Leos can be stubborn and inflexible at times. They can also be prone to arrogance and may become overly self-centered. They may have a tendency to dominate and overrule others, which can lead to conflicts in their relationships. Leos are known for their strength and bravery, but they also have a sensitive side. They can be deeply affected by criticism or rejection and may struggle with feelings of insecurity at times. Despite the innate self-assurance of Leo, Lions can be vulnerable. It is precisely this self-assurance that gives great directness and openness, but in doing so, Leo also reveals everything about him or herself. Leo has, because as Sun sign it actually contains all information and feelings already rudimentary, a unique kind of sensitivity for the other, which is also the source of his warmth to the outside world. Leo can, as it were, radiate like the Sun.

When it comes to matters of the heart, Leos are renowned for their passionate and romantic nature. They are often exceedingly generous with their time, attention, and affection, and they take great pleasure in showering their partners with gifts and adoration. Additionally, the most developed Leo types hold values such as courage, honesty, and straightforwardness in high regard, and will always stand up for others' rights to express themselves, their opinion and their talents.

In particular, Leos have a unique affinity for children, childhood, and the carefree playfulness that characterizes that stage of our life. Especially those Leos who don't place great importance on social status or decorum tend to retain this childlike outlook on life throughout their adult years, taking things "more sunny and adventurous than serious", but not out of some naivety or escapism. This Leonine feature of preserving the inner child against all odds, is often interwoven with Leonine creativity, lust for life or artistic endeavors.

Aquarians are best known for their independent and individualistic nature. They value their freedom and independence and are not afraid to express their opinions, even if it goes against the norm. They are progressive thinkers who are always looking for new and innovative ideas. Aquarians are known for their intelligence and creativity. Because they can think outside the box to find creative solutions they are great problem solvers and are always looking for new and innovative ways to approach a challenge. They are also great communicators and are able to express their ideas and opinions clearly and effectively. Aquarians can be humanitarian and altruistic with a strong desire to help others and make the world a better place.

They are natural activists and are not afraid to stand up for what they believe in, even if it means going against the status quo. They are also open-minded and accepting of others, regardless of their differences.

On the other hand, Aquarians can sometimes be emotionally detached and aloof. They may struggle with expressing their emotions, which can make them appear cold or unemotional. Additionally, they may have a tendency to rebel against authority or tradition, which can sometimes lead to conflicts in both their personal and professional lives. Some Aquarians are deeply involved in technological development and digital innovation, but may overlook the potential dangers associated with them. In some cases, they become anti-social autocrats, may hold totalitarian ideas and exhibit cold personalities. For instance, neocon-warmonger Dick Cheney played a leading role in implementing FEMA-camps across the United States.

Aquarians are known for being complex and unpredictable partners when it comes to love and relationships. They tend to prioritize intellectual connections with their partners, sometimes at the expense of emotional intimacy. Additionally, Aquarians may struggle with commitment and often require a significant amount of freedom and independence in their relationships. While independence is important, it can lead Aquarians to attract partners who also struggle with attachment and commitment, making a relation very unstable. A lot of Aquarians remain single or consciously choose this way of life.

The Leo-Aquarius axis is commonly known as the creative axis. Aquarius serves as the idea spinner and inspirer, while Leo is the artistic expresser. The two rely on each other's synergy to produce their creative output. Without Leo, Aquarius may find themselves stuck in venting ideas without producing anything tangible, or their activities and visions may lack the warmth that Leo brings. On the other hand, without Aquarius, Leo's creativity may become stagnant and repetitive, limiting their potential for growth and development. Aquarius plays a crucial role in constantly exploring and expanding horizons, which is necessary for the axis to thrive.

In terms of their approach to life, Leos tend to be more traditional and conservative in their thinking, while Aquarians are more progressive and open-minded. Leos value stability and predictability, while Aquarians are more willing to take risks and try new things. When it comes to relationships, Leos may be more focused on romance and emotional connection, while Aquarians may prioritize intellectual compatibility and independence. Leos may value traditional gender roles and may want to be the dominant partner in a relationship, while Aquarians may prefer a more equal and balanced dynamic.

SUMMARY OF THE POSITIVE QUALITIES OF LEO & AQUARIUS

LEO

Leo is the fifth astrological sign in the Zodiac, and it is represented by the Lion, reflecting the sign's emphasis on strength, leadership, and confidence. On a mundane level Leo rules over entertainment, creativity, drama, performing arts, fashion, jewelry, luxury goods, gambling, children, sports, and royalty. Here are some of the positive traits, qualities, and features associated with the zodiac sign Leo:

1. **Confidence**: Leos are known for their confidence and self-assurance. They have a strong sense of self-worth and are not afraid to take risks or stand up for themselves.
2. **Leadership**: Leos are natural leaders and often find themselves in positions of authority. They have a talent for inspiring and motivating others to achieve their goals.
3. **Creativity**: Leos are highly creative and artistic. They have a talent for self-expression and may pursue careers in the arts, fashion, or entertainment.
4. **Generosity**: Leos are generous and giving. They enjoy sharing their resources and talents with others and are often involved in charitable causes.
5. **Warmth**: Leos are warm and affectionate. They have a magnetic personality and are often surrounded by friends and admirers.
6. **Courage**: Leos are courageous and fearless. They are not afraid to take on challenges or pursue their dreams, even in the face of adversity.
7. **Loyalty**: Leos are loyal and faithful friends. They value their relationships and are often the "glue" that holds their friend group together.
8. **Charisma**: Leos have a natural charisma and charm that draws others to them. They have a talent for making people feel special and appreciated.

9. **Determination**: Leos are determined and persistent. They have a strong work ethic and are willing to put in the time and effort to achieve their goals.
10. **Optimism**: Leos have a positive and optimistic outlook on life. They believe that anything is possible and have a talent for seeing the good in people and situations.

AQUARIUS

Aquarius is the eleventh astrological sign in the Zodiac, and it is represented by the Water Bearer, reflecting the sign's emphasis on innovation, independence, and humanitarianism. On a mundane level Aquarius rules over humanitarianism, innovation, technology, social causes, astrology, aviation, space travel, electric and electronic devices, digitization, and intellectual pursuits. Here are some of the positive traits, qualities, and features associated with the zodiac sign Aquarius:

1. **Independent**: Aquarians are highly independent and value their freedom. They are not afraid to go against the norm and march to the beat of their own drum.
2. **Innovative**: Aquarians are innovative and forward-thinking. They have a talent for coming up with new and creative ideas and solutions.
3. **Humanitarian**: Aquarians are humanitarian and socially conscious. They have a strong sense of justice and are often involved in social causes and movements.
4. **Intellectual**: Aquarians are intellectual and curious. They enjoy learning and expanding their knowledge, and are often drawn to science, technology, and philosophy.
5. **Open-minded**: Aquarians are open-minded and accepting of others. They are not judgmental and are willing to listen to different perspectives and ideas.

6. **Friendly**: Aquarians are friendly and sociable. They enjoy meeting new people and making friends, and are often the life of the party.
7. **Eccentric**: Aquarians are eccentric and unconventional. They have a unique sense of style and may pursue interests or hobbies that are outside of the mainstream.
8. **Visionary**: Aquarians are visionary and forward-looking. They have a talent for seeing the big picture and are able to think long-term when making decisions.
9. **Altruistic**: Aquarians are altruistic and selfless. They are often driven by a desire to make the world a better place and may volunteer or donate to charity.
10. **Objective**: Aquarians are often objective and rational. They are able to think critically and logically, and may be drawn to careers in science or engineering.

SUMMARY OF THE NEGATIVE QUALITIES OF LEO & AQUARIUS

LEO

1. **Arrogant**: Leo can be arrogant and may have a tendency to boast or exaggerate their achievements.
2. **Self-centered**: Leo may struggle with considering the needs or perspectives of others. Leo can be egotistical and may display an exaggerated sense of me, myself and I.
3. **Domineering**: Leo can be domineering and may have a strong desire for control or leadership.
4. **Attention-seeking**: Leo can be attention-seeking and may crave validation or recognition from others.
5. **Stubborn**: Leo can be stubborn and may resist change or alternative viewpoints.
6. **Impatient**: Leo can be impatient and may struggle with waiting or delays in achieving their goals.

7. **Bossy**: Leo can be bossy and may attempt to control or micromanage those around them.

8. **Sitting on a "rusty throne"**: Leos often find great satisfaction in the recognition and praise they receive for their creative or artistic endeavors. However, this can sometimes lead them to become complacent and rely on the same techniques or styles repeatedly, inhibiting their growth and creative expression. It is important for Leos to challenge themselves and embrace new approaches in order to continue to develop their talents and produce truly innovative work.

9. **Drama queen**: Leos may have a tendency to overreact and exaggerate certain situations, which can sometimes lead to embarrassment and compromise their natural authority. To maintain a strong presence, it may be beneficial for Leos to practice restraint and consider the potential impact of their actions before reacting impulsively.

10. **Demanding**: Leo can be demanding and may expect a lot from others, which can sometimes be unrealistic or unfair.

AQUARIUS

1. **Detached**: Aquarius can be emotionally detached and may struggle with expressing or understanding their own emotions, as well as connecting with others on an emotional level.

2. **Aloof**: Aquarius can be aloof and may have a tendency to keep others at a distance, even in close relationships.

3. **Stubborn**: Aquarius can be stubborn and may have a tendency to hold onto their own opinions or ideas, even in the face of new information or evidence.

4. **Unpredictable**: Aquarius can be unpredictable and may have a tendency to change their mind or direction frequently.

5. **Rebellious**: Aquarius can be rebellious and may have a tendency to challenge authority or established norms and traditions, even if

this is not appropriate - most of the time however their rebellion is justified.

6. **Inconsistent**: Aquarius can be inconsistent and may have a tendency to flit from one idea or interest to the next without fully following through on anything.

7. **Technocracy**: Aquarius can be an advocate of transhumanism and other clinical technical dehumanizing developments that pust people towards the unnatural and artificial, thus uprooting people(s) or society.

8. **Opinionated and supporting cancel culture**: Aquarius can be opinionated and may have a tendency to form strong opinions about people or situations without fully understanding them.

9. **Judgmental or autocratic**: Aquarius can be judgmental and may have a tendency to form opinions about people or situations without fully understanding them. A typical negative Aquarius treat is a tendency towards autocracy whereby one is so full of ones own "new and progressive" conceptions that the others opinion gets nothing but a concrete wall.

10. **Impersonal**: Aquarius can be impersonal and may have a tendency to focus on ideas or concepts rather than individuals or personal relationships. The dictatorship of the group also falls under this sign.

Virgo – Pisces axis

For those born under Virgo (August 23 - September 22)
or Pisces (February 19 - March 20)

The Virgo-Pisces axis extends as it were from *singularity* to *totality*, encompassing both *specialism* and *holism*. This axis is also about the correlation of physical and spiritual health. The signs are therefore strongly linked to the psychosomatic. The Virgo-Pisces axis represents the balance between practicality and spirituality. Virgo represents practicality, organization, and analytical thinking, while Pisces represents spirituality, creativity, and intuition.

Famous people born under Virgo:
Beyoncé - September 4, 1981
Michael Jackson - August 29, 1958
Cameron Diaz - August 30, 1972
Keanu Reeves - September 2, 1964
Salma Hayek - September 2, 1966
Freddie Mercury - September 5, 1946
Blake Lively - August 25, 1987
Idris Elba - September 6, 1972
Chris Pine - August 26, 1980
Zendaya - September 1, 1996

Famous people born under Pisces:
Rihanna - February 20, 1988
Albert Einstein - March 14, 1879
Bruce Willis - March 19, 1955
Pierre-Auguste Renoir - February 25, 1841
Steve Jobs - February 24, 1955
Kurt Cobain - February 20, 1967
Eva Longoria - March 15, 1975
Drew Barrymore - February 22, 1975
Jon Bon Jovi - March 2, 1962
Elizabeth Taylor - February 27, 1932

VIRGO

As a Virgo you can improve your life substantially by integrating these Pisces qualities:

- **Compassion**: Pisces is known for their compassion and empathy, and Virgo can benefit from developing this same sense of compassion in their personal and professional relationships.
- **Increased creativity**: Virgo can benefit from integrating Pisces' imaginative and creative qualities, which can help them think outside the box and find unique solutions to problems.
- **Flexibility**: Virgo can benefit from integrating Pisces' adaptable and flexible qualities, which can help them become more open to change and more willing to take risks to create new opportunities and possibilities..
- **Intuition**: Pisces is highly intuitive and able to sense what others are feeling, and Virgo can benefit from developing this same sense of intuition in order to make better decisions and navigate complex situations.
- **Spirituality**: Pisces is often associated with spirituality and a connection to the divine, and Virgo can benefit from incorporating more of this sense of spiritual awareness and connection into their own life.
- **Sensitivity**: Pisces is known for their sensitivity and ability to pick up on subtle nuances in their environment, and Virgo can benefit from developing this same sense of sensitivity in order to better understand the needs of those around them.
- **Forgiveness and compassion**: Pisces is often able to forgive and let go of grudges, and Virgo can benefit from adopting this same sense of forgiveness in order to cultivate more positive and harmonious relationships. Pisces' compassionate nature can help Virgo become more empathetic and understanding of others, which can improve their relationships and overall well-being.

PISCES

As a Pisces you can improve your life substantially by integrating these Virgo qualities:

- **Practicality**: Virgo is known for their practicality and attention to detail, and Pisces can benefit from incorporating more of this sense of practicality into their own life in order to stay organized and focused.
- **Analytical thinking**: Virgo is often highly analytical and able to break down complex problems into smaller, more manageable parts, and Pisces can benefit from developing this same sense of analytical thinking in order to approach challenges with more clarity and focus. Pisces can also benefit from Virgo's analytical and logical approach to problem-solving.
- **Work ethic**: Virgo is often highly diligent and hardworking, and Pisces can benefit from adopting this same sense of work ethic in order to achieve their goals and make progress towards their dreams. Integrating Virgo's self-discipline can help Pisces overcome procrastination and develop greater self-control in all areas of their life.
- **Realism and finance**: Virgo is often grounded in reality and able to see things for what they truly are, and Pisces can benefit from developing this same sense of realism in order to make better decisions and navigate life with more clarity. Virgo's natural talent for managing finances can help Pisces develop better money management skills and make smarter financial decisions.
- **Health consciousness**: Virgo is often health-conscious and prioritizes self-care and wellness, and Pisces can benefit from incorporating more of this sense of self-care into their own life in order to cultivate greater physical and mental health.
- **Attention to detail**: Virgo is often highly detail-oriented and focused on precision, and Pisces can benefit from developing this

same sense of attention to detail in order to achieve greater success in their endeavors. Virgo's attention to detail can help Pisces become more focused on their goals and tasks.

- **Organizational skills**: Virgo is known for their organizational skills and ability to manage complex tasks and projects, and Pisces can benefit from adopting this same sense of organization in order to streamline their own life and pursuits.

UNDERSTANDING VIRGO & PISCES

Individuals with a strong Virgo influence tend to be diligent hard workers who possess sharp analytical skills and excel at math, planning, and organizing. They have a natural curiosity that, when combined with their analytical abilities, makes them well-suited for detective or investigative work. Virgo is known for being the most technical of all the signs.

However, one area where Virgos may struggle is with expressing and handling their own feelings and emotions, as well as those of others. Negative traits that may emerge include complaining, squeamishness, a tendency to focus only on details and miss the bigger picture, criticizing without offering solutions, neuroses, over-perfectionism, sloppiness, and a proclivity for making oneself sick to avoid obligations or responsibilities. In some cases, afflicted Virgos may seek out military, police, or control service professions that involve wearing a uniform for the wrong reasons. Uniforms are associated with negative Virgo (obey!) and Pices (uniformity for all) traits. Many Virgos work in service professions related to healthcare. Virgos may experience health issues related to the intestines, bile, nervous system, or feet. Although they may experience frequent complaints, in most cases, they typically do not reach a level of severity that is dangerous.

Differentiation is a hallmark of Virgo, but with affliction (particularly when the Centaur Cyllarus and/or the Aten-asteroid Cruithne are strong in the horoscope), this trait can turn into discrimination, racism, or xenophobia. When Virgos experience tension, it tends to manifest in the gut. Psychosynthesis is often an effective remedy for Virgos to alleviate their symptoms.

The positive Virgo personality is known for their positive traits, such as above-average intelligence, a sharp analytical mind, a sense of humor, good health, and a well-groomed fitness-body. Virgos handle their energy well, making them reliable partners and hard workers who don't put on airs. Their criticism is constructive and thoughtful, rather than impulsive.

The ultimate expression of the positive Virgo energy is the ability to live in the present while still preparing for the future, and to view service not as obedience or submission, but as a way to allow their own unique talents to flourish. This perspective recognizes that the world is full of unique individuals, each with their own talents and abilities. A positive Virgo understands this, and uses their skills to shape their own individual process.

Many successful writers have strong Virgo traits. Those who have found the greatest success often have a strong connection with the opposite sign, Pisces. This combination creates a synergy between Virgo's communicative and mercurial nature, and Pisces' inspiration and imagination. The result is an abundant and inexhaustible source of creativity that can be captured in writing. This fertile cadence creates a writing experience where the book almost writes itself. Famous examples of this pairing include Stephen King and Johann Wolfgang von Goethe.

Pisces individuals tend to lead a life that is the opposite of Virgos. They are not known for their analytical skills, but rather for their imaginative and visionary tendencies. Where Virgo loves writing as a creative medium, Pisces loves video, visual arts and music. Pisces individuals are explorers of their own inner worlds and mystical realms, often losing themselves in sleep, daydreams, and creative pursuits. They are also philosophers of the humanistic genre and mystics.

Virgos tend to be more organized, and this can often lead to controlling or over-controlling tendencies. On the other hand, Pisces individuals prefer to merge with another sphere, which requires letting go of control. If they do not let go of control, they cannot enter this other sphere. Because of this, Pisces individuals are more likely to use stimulants to enter this other world, which can range from 3D glasses to psychotropic drugs, booze, or occult techniques like lucid dreaming or theurgic magic.

The boundary between the astral world and the world of natural energies and beings is thinnest in Pisces. While Capricorn sets boundaries and Aquarius pushes them, Pisces dissolves and makes them disappear entirely. However, the challenge for Pisces individuals is returning to earthly reality. Many of them prefer to spend their days lost in film, imagery, music, or other worlds through reading or daydreaming. When this tendency becomes pathological, Pisces individuals risk missing out on fully participating in life and becoming trapped in the past. This can lead to self-harm, addiction, or a lack of self-awareness.

Pisces individuals often struggle with physical afflictions, particularly foot complaints. To avoid self-undoing, it's important for Pisces individuals to ground themselves in reality and actively engage in the world around them. The illusion of understanding how life works and being in control is just that, an illusion. One must engage with life and feel life to truly understand it.

Positive Pisces personalities show an upbeat attitude. They are often highly developed and well-read, with a great talent for creativity. They can easily distance themselves from their own zeitgeist and reality, allowing them to produce a relatively high percentage of genius artistic expression. Michelangelo Buonarroti, a highly versatile artist, architect, sculptor and poet, for example, had Sun, Moon and Mars in Pisces. Mihail Gorbachev, who defrosted the entire USSR and has been working for a better world as a humanist, environmentalist and writer ever since, had Mercury and Sun in Pisces.

Positive Pisces personalities have a deep understanding of the human drama and feel deeply for the suffering in the world. This understanding of suffering in the world unconsciously reflects their sense of mystical reality, as described by Anita Moorjani or by people after a near-death experience. They can be immensely sacrificial and engage as aid workers in places where few venture. Instead of letting life pass them by from the sidelines, they are in the middle of it.

SUMMARY OF THE POSITIVE QUALITIES OF VIRGO & PISCES

VIRGO

Virgo is the sixth astrological sign in the Zodiac, and it is represented by the Virgin, reflecting the sign's emphasis on practicality, organization, and attention to detail. On a mundane level Virgo rules over healthcare, pharmaceuticals, nutrition, science, research, analysis, organization, cleanliness, gardening, pets, and small animals. Here are some of the positive traits, qualities, and features associated with the zodiac sign Virgo:

1. **Analytical**: Virgos are analytical and logical. They have a talent for problem-solving and are able to think critically and objectively.
2. **Practical**: Virgos are practical and grounded. They have a talent for finding efficient and effective solutions to everyday problems.
3. **Organized**: Virgos are highly organized and detail-oriented. They are able to manage complex projects and tasks with ease.
4. **Reliable**: Virgos are reliable and responsible. They take their commitments seriously and can be counted on to follow through on their promises.
5. **Modest**: Virgos are modest and humble. They do not seek attention or praise for their accomplishments, but rather focus on doing their best work.
6. **Diligent**: Virgos are diligent and hardworking. They have a strong work ethic and are willing to put in the time and effort to achieve their goals.
7. **Intelligent**: Virgos are intelligent and well-read. They have a talent for absorbing and retaining information, and may pursue careers in academia or research.
8. **Meticulous**: Virgos are meticulous and precise. They have a keen eye for detail and are able to identify even the smallest errors or inconsistencies.
9. **Health-conscious**: Virgos are health-conscious and may pay close attention to their diet, exercise routine, and overall wellness.
10. **Compassionate**: Virgos are compassionate and caring. They may be drawn to careers in healthcare or social work, and often have a strong desire to help others.

PISCES

Pisces is the twelfth astrological sign in the Zodiac, and it is represented by the Fish, reflecting the sign's emphasis on intuition and empathy. On a mundane level Pisces rules over spirituality, mysticism, psychic abilities, music, poetry, theater, film, dance, addiction, healthcare, and charity. Here are some of the positive traits, qualities, and features associated with the zodiac sign Pisces:

1. **Compassion**: Pisces are deeply compassionate and empathetic. They have a strong sense of empathy and are able to connect with others on a deep emotional level.
2. **Creativity**: Pisces are highly creative and artistic. They have a talent for expressing themselves through music, art, and other forms of creative expression.
3. **Intuition**: Pisces are highly intuitive and sensitive. They have a talent for sensing the emotions and intentions of others, and are often able to see beyond the surface.
4. **Adaptability**: Pisces are highly adaptable and flexible. They are able to adjust to new situations and environments quickly and easily.
5. **Spiritual**: Pisces are deeply spiritual and often have a strong connection to the divine. They are often drawn to mystical and metaphysical subjects.
6. **Kindness**: Pisces are kind and gentle by nature. They have a warm and caring demeanor and are often seen as the "helpers" of the zodiac.
7. **Imagination**: Pisces are highly imaginative and have a rich inner life. They have a talent for creating vivid and imaginative worlds in their minds.
8. **Forgiveness**: Pisces are forgiving by nature. They are able to let go of grudges and are often able to see the good in others.
9. **Empathy**: Pisces have a strong sense of empathy and are able to connect with others on a deep emotional level. They have a talent for understanding the feelings and emotions of others.
10. **Generosity**: Pisces are generous and giving by nature. They have a desire to help others and are often willing to go out of their way to do so.

SUMMARY OF THE NEGATIVE QUALITIES OF VIRGO & PISCES

VIRGO

1. **Blind obedience**: This is the worst trait of the negative Virgo. Virgo likes to serve others, but should not waste their energy on corrupted political leaders or systems, that harm people instead of elevate them.
2. **Critical**: Virgo can be critical and may have a tendency to point out flaws or weaknesses in themselves and others, which can sometimes be discouraging or demotivating or even ruin their relations.
3. **Pessimistic**: Virgo can be pessimistic and may struggle with seeing the positive side of situations or having a hopeful outlook.
4. **Judgmental**: Virgo can be judgmental and may form opinions or make decisions based on their own biases or preconceived notions.
5. **Rigid**: Virgo can be rigid and may struggle with flexibility or adaptability in new situations.
6. **Overly analytical:** Virgo can be overly analytical and may have a tendency to overthink or obsess about details.
7. **Nitpicky**: Virgo can get too much absorbed in detail and may set high standards for themselves and others, which can sometimes be unrealistic. Virgo can be nitpicky and may focus on small, insignificant details at the expense of the bigger picture.
8. **Neurotic**: Virgos' perfectionism can lead them to set extremely high standards for themselves and others, which may be unrealistic and result in a chronic state of edginess. This can, in turn, lead to neurotic health problems.
9. **Obsessive**: Virgo can be obsessive and may have a tendency to fixate on certain ideas or behaviors.
10. **Messy**: Positive Virgins are hygienic and tidy, while negative Virgins can manifest a negative Pisces pattern of total sloppiness.

PISCES

1. **Indecisive**: Pisces can be indecisive and may struggle with making decisions, especially when faced with complex or conflicting information.

2. **Escapist**: Pisces can be prone to escapism and may have a tendency to avoid or ignore difficult situations or emotions. This trait can become a serious obstacle in their social life.

3. **Chasing illusions**: Pisces can be idealistic and may have a tendency to set unrealistic expectations for themselves and others.

4. **Oversensitive**: Pisces can be oversensitive and may have a tendency to take things personally or to be easily hurt by criticism.

5. **Gullible**: Pisces can be gullible and may have a tendency to believe things without questioning them or doing their own research.

6. **Passive**: Pisces can be passive and may have a tendency to go along with the opinions or decisions of others, rather than asserting themselves.

7. **Moody**: Pisces can be moody and may have a tendency to experience emotional highs and lows, sometimes without clear cause.

8. **Self-pitying**: Pisces can be self-pitying and may have a tendency to dwell on their own problems or misfortunes.

9. **Irresponsible**: Pisces can be irresponsible and may have a tendency to neglect their duties or obligations, especially if they find them boring or uninteresting.

10. **Disorganized**: Pisces can be disorganized and may have a tendency to struggle with planning, time management, and keeping their physical space tidy.

PAPER BOOKS

VAMzzz Publishing is a company that preserves historical occult books and produces new and revised editions in various categories such as Magic & Witchcraft, Secret Rites & Societies, Demonology, Celtic & Mythology, and New Astrology.

Our books are written by highly qualified academic researchers or experts in specific fields of esoteric knowledge, craft, or practice. Many of the revised titles include a Post Scriptum with additional information about the author or subject.

Our reproductions of classic texts differ from others in two important ways. Firstly, we have chosen not to rely on OCR (Optical Character Recognition) technology, as we believe that this often results in poor quality books that are littered with typos and other errors. Secondly, in cases where the original text contains images, such as portraits, maps, or sketches, we have taken great care to preserve the quality of these illustrations, ensuring that they accurately reflect the original artefact. By preserving and sharing these works, we can gain a deeper understanding of our cultural heritage and the rich history of human thought and creativity that has come before us.

In addition to publishing books, VAMzzz Publishing also offers FREE articles on various occult topics, including Afro-American magic, folklore, and New Astrology on our blog. You are welcome to visit vamzzz.com/blog and explore these subjects further.

VAMzzz Publishing
P.O. Box 3340
1001 AC Amsterdam
The Netherlands
vamzzz@protonmail.com
www.vamzzz.com

Centaurs, Damocloids & Scattered Disc Objects
Asteroids in Astrology 1
by Benjamin Adamah, 162 pages, Hardcover
ISBN 9789492355409 (Professional literature)
Challenging the astrological status quo, this book discusses the fascinating astrological significance of no less than 85 Centaurs and Centaur related asteroids like Scattered Disc Objects (SDOs) & Detached Objects, Damocloids, retrograde Asteroids and (ex-) Comets. Centaurs are of major psychological importance, and as is the case with the first discovered Centaur Chiron, most of them are about healing and psycho-synthesis.

Plutinos
Asteroids in Astrology 2
by Benjamin Adamah, 126 pages, Hardcover
ISBN 9789492355522 (Professional literature)
Astrological research points out that most Plutinos, like their godfather Pluto, exert a compelling force in both personal and mundane horoscopes. They are radical, transforming, confronting, they penetrate the darkness, the blur, or daily life patterns and have a Scorpio-like preference for what you might call soul-mining. They trigger the awareness of slumbering patterns in the depths of our souls and force us to face the truth.

Spirit Beings in European Folklore 1
Ireland, England, Wales, Cornwall, Scotland, Isle of Man, Orkney's, Hebrides, Faeroe, Iceland, Norway, Sweden and Denmark
by Benjamin Adamah, 250 pages, Paperback,
ISBN 9789492355553
This book catalogs the mysterious creatures of Ireland, the Isle of Man, England, Wales, Cornwall, Scotland, Hebrides, Orkneys, Faroe Islands, Iceland, Norway, Sweden and Denmark. For centuries, the peoples of these regions have influenced each other in many ways, including their mythologies and folklore.

Spirit Beings in European Folklore 2

Germany, Austria, Alpine regions, Switzerland, Netherlands, Flanders, Luxembourg, Lithuania, Latvia, Estonia, Finland, Jewish influences
by Benjamin Adamah, 256 pages, Paperback, ISBN 9789492355560

Compendium 2 covers the German-speaking parts of Central Europe, the Low Countries, the Baltic region and Finland. Via the Ashkenazi Jews, spirit beings from the Middle East entered Central European culture, which are also included.

Spirit Beings in European Folklore 3

Russia, Belarus, Ukraine, Poland, Romania, Hungary, Bulgaria, Czechia, Slovenia, Serbia, Croatia, Albania, Georgia, Turkish regions, Roma-culture
by Benjamin Adamah, 246 pages, Paperback, ISBN 9789492355577

Compendium 3 offers an overview of the mysterious, sometimes beautiful and often shadowy entities of the Slavic countries, the Balkans, the Carpathians, Albania, Georgia, and the Turkish and Romani peoples. Many types of Vampires and vampiric Revenants are included – in their original state and purged of later applied disinformation.

Spirit Beings in European Folklore 4

France, Brittany, Wallonia, Portugal, Italy, South Tyrol, Malta, Greece, Spain – Basque Country, Asturias, Catalonia, Cantabria, Galicia, Valencia
by Benjamin Adamah, 250 pages, Paperback, ISBN 9789492355584

Compendium 4 covers an area that starts with Wallonia and continues via France and the Pyrenees, through the Iberian Peninsula, to Italy and Greece. This results in a very diverse and colourful collection of spirit beings, due to the many included Basque nature-spirits or Ireluak, the Spanish Duendes, the Celtic spirits of Brittany, the prankster Italian Folletti and the creatures from Greece.